MAPLE KING

Maple King
The Making of a Maple Syrup Empire

Matthew M. Thomas

Maple King: The Making of a Maple Syrup Empire

© 2018 Matthew M. Thomas

All rights reserved. No parts of this publication may be reproduced, stored in a retrieval system, or transmitted in any form or by any means, electronic, mechanical, photocopying, recording, or otherwise, without the prior written permission of the copyright owner except in the case of brief quotations embodied in critical reviews and certain other noncommercial uses permitted by copyright law.

For information on getting permission for reprints and excerpts, contact www.maplesyruphistory.com

ISBN: - 13 978-1986277211
ISBN: - 10 1986277216

First Printing Edition 2018

Printed in the United States of American by CreateSpace an Amazon.com company.

Front cover image and cover design by author. Lower front cover image courtesy of Cary family archives, rear cover image courtesy of Tom Olson and the New England Maple Museum.

Available from Amazon.com and other retail outlets.

Dedicated To

Stephen Jones
The strength in your interest
and passion for the George C. Cary story
inspired me to carry this story through to completion

and

Charlie Welcome
Your attention to the history of the Cary
Company in the mid-century years brought to
light a whole new chapter of the story

and

Daniel Gade
For always opening my eyes and mind
to think differently about maple history
and encouraging me to get to know Vermont

CONTENTS

Preface
Acknowledgements

1 Introduction 1
2 Formation of the Kingdom 15
3 Expansion of the Kingdom 45
4 Growing the King's Army 81
5 The King is Dead 101
6 A New Empire in a New Era 123
7 Legacy of a Maple King 145

Notes 151

Preface

To those interested in Vermont history or the history of the maple sugar and syrup industry, the general story of George C. Cary is fairly well-known. A travelling salesman in the 1880s in Vermont finds himself stuck with hundreds of pounds of maple sugar that he doesn't know what to do with. He lucks upon the idea of selling it to tobacco companies for the making of chewing tobacco and cigarettes. The idea is a hit. He moves into the maple sugar business, and a few years later is the single largest handler of maple sugar in the world. His maple empire continues to grow but the challenges of sitting on an enormous surplus of maple sugar during the financial crisis of the Great Depression lead to Cary's personal bankruptcy and unexpected death. On its face, it's a compelling story, but was there more to it than that? What do we really know about George Cary, the many other avenues of the maple industry in which he was involved, and the effects of his influence on the maple industry? In short, what was his legacy? Ultimately, answering these questions are what led me to write this book, but that wasn't so clear from the beginning.

When explaining my research and work on this book, people frequently asked, "how did you get interested in George Cary and maple sugaring; you're not from Vermont?" Well, that's a good question and not exactly easy to answer. It all began in 1996 when I was working as the Tribal Archaeologist for the Lac du Flambeau Band of Lake Superior Chippewa Indians in northern Wisconsin. While conducting archaeological surveys for the tribe in advance of planned projects like timber sales, housing developments, and water and sewer improvements, we repeatedly were finding collections of old metal food cans and associated items in the woods that didn't look like other historic sites we were used to seeing. They were different from homesteads and logging camps and other known historic era sites made by people in the last 150 years. After a little asking around and looking at site records from the surveys of other researchers in northern Wisconsin and adjacent Michigan, it became clear to those of us working in the tribal historic preservation office that we were probably seeing the remains of maple sugaring activities.

For a young, inexperienced (I'll admit that now) archaeologist like myself, these kinds of sites were a new and interesting challenge to understand. A little more poking around showed that, outside of largely basic recording and documenting of these sugaring sites, there really hadn't been much research done to interpret these camps and material remains found at these sorts of sites or present them in a broader historic context. So, my colleagues in the tribal historic preservation office and I embarked on a project to document as many sites on the reservation as we could and describe and explain what we found. But for us to understand anything about the material remains from the activities related to making maple sugar we first had to learn about the history and process of maple sugaring.

And that is where George C. Cary first became known to me. It was in reading the 1993 book *Sweet Maple* by Lawrence and Martin that I first read the story of Cary and his maple empire. While it was interesting, and his name cropped up a few more times during my extensive background research on Native American maple sugaring, it wasn't really that directly connected to what we were dealing with on the reservation. We finished that project in 1999 and produced a nice report[1], published an article in an obscure regional archaeology journal[2], and presented our results at a major archaeology conference[3], but for the most part I really didn't think I'd do much more with the maple sugaring topic. I moved on from my job with the tribe and was living in Montana. But as many people can tell you, the world of maple sugaring is a funny thing and it grabs a hold of you and doesn't let go. Some call it maple fever and I had caught it.

Quite by accident I was put in touch with a professor of landscape architecture in nearby Moscow, Idaho who had written a paper about historic maple sugaring sites in the forest landscape while she was a forest ecology graduate student in Upper Michigan. She was interested in my recent work and in possibly collaborating with me on a project to look at these historic sugaring sites from the perspective of historic landscapes and landscape change. We met, hit it off, and started to work up an idea for a paper, right about the time she accepted a new faculty position at the University of Wisconsin in Madison. Madison was an interesting connection she and I had in common. She had done her undergraduate studies in Madison and I had completed my master's degree and started on my Doctorate in Anthropology at UW-Madison before leaving to take the above-mentioned position as tribal archaeologist. I initially thought that her move from Moscow to Madison was going to put a kink in our collaboration, but she surprised me with an offer I couldn't refuse. She suggested I come to Madison to earn a Ph.D. from the Institute of Environmental Studies and work with her on an expanded version of our historic maple sugaring landscapes project as a fully funded Research Assistant.

In the fall of 2000 I returned to Madison and dived into learning anything and everything I could about the history and process of maple sugaring. While Madison was and is an amazing place to do historical research and the State of Wisconsin has a strong maple syrup industry, I needed to go to the heart of the maple sugaring world to really understand the history of this topic. This led me to take several trips to Vermont, New York and Quebec, where I visited maple museums, spent time in libraries and archives, visited maple festivals, and met with a variety of current and retired maple producers and industry professionals. Along the way I kept coming across stories, photos, and references to George Cary and the Cary Maple Sugar Company. This included my first review of the Cary Papers in the archives at the Fairbanks Museum and Planetarium in St. Johnsbury, which I filed away as interesting, but not immediately relevant to the story of the history of maple sugaring in the Upper Midwest about which I was investigating and planning to write about.

In some circles I had become something of an expert on the archaeological remains of maple sugaring sites and artifacts in the western Great Lakes region, and while working on my dissertation received a request from a friend and archaeologist with the Chequamegon-Nicolet National Forest to come and look at a site that had them a little perplexed. It looked like a sugaring camp, but it contained hundreds of sections of metal tubing stacked in piles which was puzzling to Forest Service staff. I visited the site and immediately recognized the metal tubing as segments of the Brower Pipeline system that I had seen on display in maple sugaring museums in Croghan, New York and Pittsford, Vermont. Wanting to know more, I dug back into my research files and began to look for everything I could find on the Brower Pipeline which soon led me back to George Cary who had been an active user and proponent of the pipeline. Being a curious researcher, whose interest was piqued by Cary's connection to the pipeline, I then wanted to learn more about Cary and began gathering information on Cary both from the library in Madison and on my research trips to New England, and even wrote a short article about the site with the metal tubing in Wisconsin.[4]

Shortly after completing my dissertation[5] and moving with my wife to Washington, D.C., I had some time on my hands and made another research trip to Vermont. While pouring over the Cary Papers in the Fairbanks Museum in St. Johnsbury with their archivist, we began discussing where exactly Cary's sugarbush was located in the woods of nearby North Danville. At the time I only had a passing idea of where Cary's farm and sugarbush were located in North Danville when the archivist said, "well, would you like to go visit it? A friend of mine has a Bed and Breakfast up there and I think that was part of the Cary sugarbush. There is an old sugarhouse in the woods behind the farm." That got my attention fast, to which I replied, "really, when could you show me?" "How about after lunch?" she replied. "You got it!", I said. In walking up the road behind the Broadview Farm Bed and Breakfast, I never really expected to be surprised, but I was shocked and giddy with what I saw. It was one of those little moments when a researcher sort of feels like they found a long lost hidden city. In front of me was a large red and white trimmed sugarhouse with "Cary Maple Sugar Co." painted in large, fading, three-foot tall letters along the outer wall. "I know this sugarhouse!" I explained. "I'll show you an old picture of it when we get back to the Museum."

The photo above was one of my favorite images of a Cary sugarhouse and was one that I certainly never expected to actually see in person. That got me wondering about what other Cary sugarhouses might still be around and what was contained in other parts of this extensive sugarbush formerly operated by Cary. I then spent an afternoon driving around the roads of North Danville to get a feel for the landscape. I had driven these roads before, generally curious about Cary on an earlier visit, but I had a new sense of purpose this time. Seeing the plastic tubing of a modern sugarbush in the woods not far from the earlier sugarhouse discovery, I pulled down their drive to both buy some syrup and to ask what they might know about Cary. That is when I met Stephen and Diane Jones, the owners of Sugar Ridge Farm. To say it was a fortuitous day would be an understatement. Sugar Ridge Farm was making maple syrup in the same sugarbush and sugarhouse as George Cary. Moreover, there was a log cabin on their property that appeared in a series of photographs associated with Cary. These photos documented an effort by Cary to show examples of the evolution of the sugaring process from Native American methods, to Yankee sugaring, up through the then modern methods of metal pails and the above-mentioned Brower Pipeline. Steve Jones was as excited to talk with me about Cary and his sugarbush as I was excited to talk to him. Steve led me all over the woods and buildings and we shared a lot of information that day and agreed to keep in touch and meet again, which we did the following summer. One item we asked each other about was reference to a silent film that Cary supposedly made, but neither of us had ever seen it or knew if it still existed.

A few years later I returned to the interesting topic of the Brower Pipeline System and I travelled to New York and Vermont to learn everything I could about the pipeline. This included visits with the descendants of Jacob Brower, the pipeline's inventor, and a further look at George Cary as the pipeline promoter, eventually resulting in a more detailed article on the history of the Brower Pipeline[6], but also deepened my understanding of the history of George Cary. In the process it fueled my desire to find the mysterious Cary silent film.

And find the film I did, later that year. In 1927 George Cary hired husband and wife photographers and filmmakers Harry and Alice Richardson from Newport, Vermont to make a silent film presenting the technological history of maple sugar making. Three eras of maple production are depicted in the film; Native American maple sugar making, nineteenth century Euro-American sugar making, and what was at that time modern, twentieth century production methods. As is discussed in Chapter Four, the film, and still photographs that accompany it, was largely shot in Cary's North Danville sugarbush and features the Cary sugarhouses, as well as the log cabin still standing in the Jones' Sugar Ridge Farm sugarbush. As I discovered, an original copy of the motion picture still on its original and very volatile silver nitrate film was found and donated in 1997 to Northeast Historic Film (NHF) by Philippe Beaudry of Longueuil, Quebec. Northeast Historic Film is a non-profit film repository in Bucksport, Maine, who luckily for me had begun posting a catalog of their collections online. In discovering the existence of the film, which had been converted to VHS at the time of donation to NHF for safer handling, I arranged for the film to be transferred from VHS to digital for viewing online and on video disc. I also prepared a summary for NHF of the history of the making of the film, based on newspaper articles and other historic sources.[7]

Shortly after discovering the Cary silent film, I embarked on a new career path, with other interests beginning to take up my time. My research on Cary was set aside, although my interest in Cary, and my maple fever affliction, never ceased. Clearly, I had collected a significant amount of information on Cary and examined his story from a number of different angles and eventually I asked myself if I thought there was enough material in the George Cary story for a book? Other writers and books like Lawrence and Martin's *Sweet Maple*, Betty Ann Lockhart's *Maple Sugarin' In Vermont: A Sweet Story*, and Peggy Pearl's *A Brief History of St. Johnsbury*, told portions of George Cary's story in various iterations, but my research had told me there was a lot more to say and explain. The story of George Cary and the Cary Maple Sugar Company did not end with his bankruptcy and death. Moreover, there was also a rich history of photos, images, and illustrations related to Cary and all his many dealings with the maple industry that remained unpublished. In fact, over the years I myself had amassed a decent collection of postcards and historic items like booklets and pamphlets related to Cary and the Maple Grove Candies company. Yes, I told myself, there was enough for a book but there were still some holes in my research and more work needed to be done.

One question I always had was whether there were any living descendants of George Cary that may have something to share in the form of stories or photos or other materials. That question led me on a search that ultimately was successful in locating two Cary granddaughters, now in their 70s. Unfortunately, George Cary had passed on before their births and they were never able to meet their grandfather in person. Time has passed such that I was not able to find any individuals that had personally met George Cary; however, I was able to interview Charlie Welcome, a former Cary Company employee and the son-in-law of Edward Boylan who ran the Cary Company from the 1930s to 1953. Fortunately, Mr. Welcome had also compiled an unpublished history of his own of the Cary Company, which helped me greatly in understanding the company in the years after Cary's death.[8]

In addition to examining as much of the written record I could find on Cary, I also had the pleasure of being able to tour the original Cary Company factory and Maple Grove Candies building now operated by Maple Grove Farms in St. Johnsbury. Seeing these places from the inside out helped me develop a deeper understanding of their place in this story. Similarly, I was introduced to the current owners of the stately home Cary built on Main Street in St. Johnsbury and was shown how they have been painstakingly working to carefully restore the interior to its original elegance.

Visiting spaces and places like the Cary factory, Cary sugarhouses, and Cary home has always been important to me in developing a sense of place in discovering and understanding history. Perhaps my initial academic training and profession as an archaeologist and historic preservationist has led me to have a strong interest in understanding the material remains of the past and seeing how they tie people together with each other and with places and landscapes. As a result, my research and presentation in this book rely heavily on the use of imagery, photos, artifacts, and maps in telling the story and assist the reader in developing a visual narrative in their own minds much as I have.

Acknowledgements

Researching and writing a book like this over many years and with the use of resources from many archives, libraries, and museums cannot be done without the support, assistance and goodwill of a small army of people.

Above all, a colossal thank you to Jennifer Eberlien, my wife and my biggest supporter. You've put up with so much and made every bit of this possible and I can never express how much I love you for it.

A very special thanks to a trio of always friendly and helpful experts in St. Johnsbury, namely Pat Swartz, archivist at the Fairbanks Museum and Planetarium, Shara McCaffrey at the St. Johnsbury Athenaeum, and Peggy Pearl at the St. Johnsbury History and Heritage Center. Over many years and multiple visits, all three were untiring in their interest and assistance with my many Cary related questions. I could not have written this without their knowledge and help navigating the collections in their respective institutions. Additional thanks to Connie Gallagher at the Bailey Howe Library of the University of Vermont and Paul Carnahan at the Vermont Historical Society for their assistance. Additional thank-yous to Tom Olson of the New England Maple Museum, and Lillian Rider of the Lennoxville-Ascot Historical & Museum Society in Sherbrooke, Quebec for access to images in their collections.

Mary Lou Curran, and Nancy Cary Aldrich were kind enough to share stories and access to photos of the grandfather George C. Cary. I hope they feel I have done his story justice. Molly Newell, Joe Newell, Stephen and Diane Jones, and Maurice Zabarsky took the time to answer my many questions and share their piece of the Cary story. Charlie Welcome deserves a special nod for taking the time to craft a history of the Cary Company many years ago and then walking me through the story that was between the lines. Mark Bigelow and Phil Ann Jenkins at Maple Grove Farms helped with questions and shared historic material relating the company, including an enjoyable and educational tour of the Cary Company facilities now run by Maple Grove Farms.

All my research trips to Vermont were made that much more special and enjoyable through the gracious hospitality, conversation, friendship and good wine of Daniel and Mary Gade. Thanks to you I always looked forward to travel to Burlington.

Financial assistance for various aspects of the research was provided by a McIntire-Stennis Grant from the University of Wisconsin and the National Science Foundation.

The editorial assistance provided by Jen Eberlien, Peg Billings, and Kim Whippy went a long way towards making this a cleaner, coherent, and hopefully more readable publication.

There are other names I have surely overlooked or forgotten. My apologies to those folks. Any errors, overstatements, understatements or omissions are solely my own.

1

Introduction

"The history of the development of the strictly modern market for maple goods in this country, to all intents and purposes, is the story of the Cary Maple Sugar Company of St. Johnsbury, VT".

- John A. Hitchcock (1928) *Economics of the Farm Manufacture of Maple Syrup and Sugar*[9]

To most modern consumers of pure maple syrup, their syrup is bought in a glass jar from the shelves of their neighborhood grocery store with a label that probably says it is a product of Canada and the United States. For commercial producers of maple syrup in the United States and Canada, most of the syrup made in their sugarbushes and sugarhouses each spring is packaged into large metal or plastic barrels or drums and sold to a handful of companies and cooperatives. It is those few companies and cooperatives who then blend the syrup of many producers into a uniform flavor, color, consistency, and grade and package it for sale on local grocery store shelves across North America and beyond.

The maple syrup business didn't always work this way. In fact, it was maple sugar, in a hard packed or granulated form, rather than liquid maple syrup, which dominated maple production in the nineteenth century. Even then, the market for maple products was slim and predominantly local.[10] The late 1800s and early 1900s were a time when farmers in the maple-producing regions were largely on their own to produce, market, and sell their maple products, mostly through direct sales to the consumer or a local grocer. However, at the end of the nineteenth century, working out of the small Vermont town of St. Johnsbury, George C. Cary and his Cary Maple Sugar Company introduced a whole new approach to the processing and marketing of maple products.

Figure 1.1: Portrait and signature of George C. Cary (Stone 1929).

This new approach forever altered the scales of production and modernized the entire structure of the maple sugar and syrup industry (Figure 1.1). The majority of maple sugar and maple syrup in this era was produced in New England, in contrast to today, where Quebec, Canada dominates production.[11] By changing and controlling the landscape of maple production over the late nineteenth and early twentieth centuries, George Cary was bestowed with the grandiose title of Maple King and the village of St. Johnsbury became known as the Maple Sugar Capitol of the World.[12]

The Late Nineteenth Century Maple Sugaring Landscape

Maple sugaring was an ancillary springtime activity of many individual farm families in the 1800s across the hardwood forests of New England, New York and adjacent Ontario and Quebec. Carried out at a time in the year when little other activity was occurring on the farm, sugaring was a welcome seasonal pursuit that yielded valuable cash returns.[13]

Figure 1.2: Image from 1929 cover of *The Vermonter* magazine with George C. Cary at center working with oxen in his North Danville sugarbush.

Sugaring was one of many food gathering or food producing activities engaged in as part of the annual cycle of the farm or rural homestead.

Unlike larger producers today, in the nineteenth and early twentieth centuries, it was unheard of to find someone solely focused on the making of maple sugar as their farm's primary economic activity. Sugarmakers of this time rarely tapped more than 1000 trees at a time. Instead, the taps in most sugarbushes were counted in the hundreds. Gathering sap from the maple trees each spring was carried out by hand and with the use of oxen or work horses (Figure 1.2). Sap was boiled in large, wood-fired evaporators in simple sugarhouses scattered amongst the maple-covered hills. Despite the limited scale of most nineteenth century sugarbushes by today's standards, the sale of maple sugar was a reliable and welcome source of cash in advance of the next growing season.

Although North American maple sugaring production peaked in 1865 in terms of absolute pounds of sugar, maple sugar's popularity as a sweetener among consumers was losing out to refined white table sugar made from sugar cane. The lighter flavor and color, and more reliable consistency of refined cane sugar was increasingly preferred by consumers. By the end of the Civil War the cost of refined cane sugar had come down in price such that it was either the same or lower than that of maple sugar. Customers preferred the consistent quality and delicate taste of and consistent quality of refined sugar. Moreover, the refined cane sugar industry was more stable and efficient than the maple sugar industry, ultimately out-competing maple sugar on price.[14]

In this post-Civil War era, changes in food packaging, advertising, and shipping of consumer goods were opening a plethora of new markets and opportunities for movement and sales of food and farm products to home consumers. Enterprising salesmen such as Patrick J. Towle of Towle's Log Cabin Syrup Company, recognized that some consumers were not as fond of the strong flavor of pure maple syrup and began marketing blended table syrups, combining pure maple syrup with cane syrup to produce a thicker syrup with a lighter taste at a fraction of the cost of 100% pure maple syrup. In the 1880s regional and national brands of blended syrups began to appear on the market. In the coming decades these blended syrup companies poured money into the promotion of their brands and ideas on how to use their products, advertising in many of the new national magazines. These advertisements were instrumental in solidifying the idea of table syrup as a breakfast topping for pancakes, waffles, and French Toast.[15]

Some sugarmakers recognized the shrinking market for maple sugar and took advantage of the growing syrup market. These producers began to shift their focus to production of maple syrup as a specialty or high-valued gourmet food for the table. There was also a growing understanding of the increasing demand for syrup packaged, shipped, and sold in smaller and more conveniently sized metal and sometimes glass containers. New packaging permitted the rise of canned and bottled syrups and advertising promoted new uses for this product opening more markets further away from the producing regions. Railroads in turn made it easier to get syrup from producers to blenders and consumers and across ever-greater distances. However, not all producers were as keen to shift from sugar to syrup.

Even with new and developing markets for maple syrup in the late nineteenth century, not all syrup was of a quality or grade considered acceptable for sale as table syrup. At the same time, not all producers wanted to be troubled with packaging and selling syrup in smaller containers direct to consumers. The transition away from the production of bulk maple sugar to the production of maple syrup for the home table was not easy for all producers, and especially so for the less progressive farms of New England, New York, and adjacent Quebec and Ontario. Not all sugarmakers were equipped for processing sap as quickly as possible or in applying more careful methods when boiling and finishing. These methods were required to produce the medium colored and flavored syrup desired by many consumers, as opposed to a dark and heavy flavored syrup. Grading of syrup was not yet standardized or required by the industry or government regulators at this time, although there was a general understanding among maple producers of a perceived higher quality and greater worth of lighter sugar and syrup.

Syrup consumers have instead chosen to buy what their palates prefer and not what they are told is premium syrup.

There are numerous printed guides and government bulletins available from the late nineteenth and early twentieth centuries that provide advice on how to operate a sugarbush and how to make maple sugar and syrup, but these guide books are curiously lacking in any discussion of what to do with the syrup and sugar once it has been made. It was as if there was an assumption that farmers needed advice about the maple production process but then everyone just "knew" how to sell and market their products, when in fact that was hardly the case at all. Furthermore, many of these guides took a very negative approach to selling maple products to individuals or companies known as packers or dealers. Packers were people and companies that bought bulk sugar and bulk syrup at a lower price in high volume. They then packaged it for re-sale to consumers or converted the sugar and syrup into blended syrups or flavoring for other products. As this story tells, George C. Cary became the biggest maple sugar packer of them all (Figure 1.3).

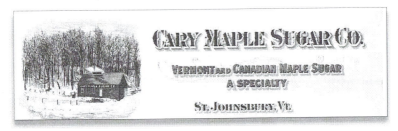

Figure 1.3: Cary Maple Sugar Company Letterhead, circa 1918.

During the early years of maple syrup becoming a condiment and table item, it was not uncommon for less scrupulous packers to blend pure maple syrup with cane or corn syrup and label the product as pure maple syrup, a process known as adulteration. As noted above, others, such as Towle's Log Cabin Syrup, were up front in sharing that their syrup was a blend. Because of the problems with some blenders falsely labeling their syrup as pure maple syrup, the syrup and sugar buyers and packers, whether or not they were lying about the contents of their products, were often viewed rather negatively as adulterators. There was a perception that packers were, and still are, less legitimate because they were not working to specifically sell pure maple syrup, as if there was some sort of greater virtue to selling or engaging in direct sales of only 100% pure maple syrup. Likewise, it has been suggested that there was an idea or ideal that real maple sugar and syrup only came directly from farms and imitation or phony maple products came from a factory.[16]

In reality, packers like Cary presented the maple producer with a greater market for their crop, often buying the lower quality portion of their year's production and leaving the premium syrup for the producer to sell at a higher price to their preferred customers. It wasn't just larger producers who sold bulk syrup and sugar to Cary; even the smaller producer took advantage of unloading extra sugar and syrup, especially in years of particularly good sugaring. After first meeting their home consumption needs and saving their best syrup for direct sales in smaller quantities like pints, quarts, half and full gallons, what was "left over" was sold to Cary.[17] Some producers eventually focused on selling the majority or even entirety of their crop, minus what they saved for home use, to packers like Cary and not bothering with marketing or direct sales.

The role of packers hasn't received much attention in the historical literature. In a recent book that explores the many meanings of maple, author Michael Lange points out the less romantic side of commodities, which includes grouping or mixing of a food item into a single anonymous product.[18] With commodities or the commodification of a food item there is a middleman or processor added to the mix, creating a further separation between the producer and the consumer. This happens with any commodity, including bulk maple syrup and sugar. By removing the more personal and direct interaction between producer and consumer, commodification in turn often results in a more generic presentation and marketing of the product. In the case of the Cary Company, most of the maple sugar and syrup they handled was going into the processing of tobacco products, so for the early years of the company there was less of a focus on developing that romantic image of sugaring or connecting with the syrup consumers.

It was with this broader context that George Cary arrived on the scene, albeit quite by accident, as explained in greater detail in Chapter Two. Cary's path to becoming the largest buyer and seller of bulk maple sugar and maple syrup in history was neither planned nor immediate, but it was novel and remarkably effective. Rather than treating maple products as food items as had always been treated, Cary focused on using maple sugar as a flavoring agent in the curing and processing of tobacco. In doing so, Cary created and grew a market for all grades and qualities of maple sugar and syrup, especially lower quality products and darker grades, with bulk purchases that maple producers would otherwise have had a difficult time selling as table sugar or table syrup. As early as 1905 Cary was said to be buying about 80 percent of the maple sugar produced in Vermont, and by 1928 Cary was buying 70 percent of the maple syrup made in Vermont.[19]

Chapter Three of this book recounts how Cary's wealth and power as an industry magnate grew. With his growing influence and control, he was not content to simply focus on the buying and selling of maple sugar. Cary also had significant financial and leadership roles in supporting the development of other maple related endeavors, such as Maple Grove Candies (the precursor to today's Maple Grove Farms), the ill-fated Brower Maple Sap Pipeline, and the expansion of the Towle's Log Cabin Syrup company outside its mid-western roots. Cary began his involvement with the Log Cabin Company as one of the earliest suppliers of maple sugar for its blended table syrup. Cary was also a member of the Log Cabin Board of Directors and directly instrumental in the decision to locate a Log Cabin bottling plant in St. Johnsbury. The co-location of the Cary Maple Sugar Company and the Towle's Maple Products Company in St. Johnsbury did not go without notice as demonstrated in Edward T. Fairbanks 1914 comment that with the Log Cabin and Cary "sugar business (together) aggregating two million dollars annually, this town is at the present the largest maple sugar market in the world".[20]

That St. Johnsbury deserved the title of Maple Sugar Capital of the World, with the Cary Company at the helm, was demonstrated when a housewife in Arizona in the 1930s wanted to place an order for pure maple syrup, but did not know where to send it, so she addressed her envelope with the words "100% Pure Maple Syrup, Vermont".

Figure 1.4: Envelope of letter for Maple Capital (image from Highland Maple recipe booklet – Author's Collection).

Receiving the letter, the U.S. Postal Service forwarded the order to St. Johnsbury and the Cary Company, since in their mind that was the most logical place to fulfill her request (Figure 1.4).[21]

Cary's success and growth in St. Johnsbury brought new attention and wealth to the village. For much of the nineteenth century, St. Johnsbury was traditionally known as the manufacturing home of the Fairbanks Scale Company and to the well-known Fairbanks family who were the town's leading citizens, with Erastus Fairbanks serving as Governor of Vermont from 1860 to 1861. The arrival and rise of the Cary Company brought a new name, new wealth, new employment, and a new focus of attention for St. Johnsbury. The growth of the Cary

Company in the village also meant the appearance of new and modern manufacturing facilities in an otherwise aging New England mill town, as discussed in Chapters Three and Four.

George Cary was a huge supporter and investor in the growth and incorporation of Maple Grove Candies in St. Johnsbury, later named just Maple Grove and more recently Maple Grove Farms of Vermont. Cary provided the financing for Maple Grove Candies to expand production and operations in the former Fairbanks mansion in the village. In later years George Cary led the way for his company to purchase Maple Grove Candies and combine it with the Cary Maple Sugar Company, only further solidifying both his and St. Johnsbury's roles as the leaders of the maple world in the early twentieth century. As the recognized leader in the maple industry, Cary used his resources to support and spread the word about new technological innovations for the industry, such as the Brower Pipeline System, as well as to promote the industry to a wider audience. As recounted in Chapter Four, Cary arranged for the creation of a silent film, shot in his sugarbush and plant, chronicling the history of the maple industry. Cary was also a leading proponent and participant in the Vermont Maple Sugar Special, a train that for several years traveled the eastern United States and Canada to promote the many home-grown products of the state of Vermont.

Cary's influence and commerce were international in breadth and extended into Quebec. Cary bought nearly as much maple syrup in Quebec as he did in the United States and established a nearly identical factory to his St. Johnsbury operation in Lennoxville, Quebec. The eventual control of the vast majority of the maple sugar market by the Cary Company essentially allowed Cary to set the price for all bulk maple products throughout New England and Quebec since few of the other packers and dealers could afford to under-cut Cary's prices. Dissatisfaction with Cary's perceived monopoly and the price controls and rates Cary was offering led to the formation of a number of cooperatives both in the U.S. and Canada in response. Most notable of these cooperatives, as outlined in Chapter Five, is the Citadelle

Cooperative in Quebec, which still exists and attributes its origins to a decision to work together and against George Cary. Ironically, the Quebec maple industry today is under great scrutiny for the imposition of state sponsored monopoly and price controls at the hands of Fédération des producteurs acéricoles du Québec, something not unlike the de facto controls imposed on Quebec producers by the Cary Company 100 years before.[22]

Telling the Cary Story

Much has been written about maple sugaring and the traditions and lore of the sugarbush, often painting a nostalgic picture of rural life in the north woods. In contrast, this book is a decidedly unromantic account of the maple industry in years past. Instead, it is a more detailed look at the how the maple industry as a business developed in the early part of the last century. As the title of the book implies, the focus of the book is on the life and role of George Cary in shaping the maple industry, but Cary was just the beginning of the story. The Cary story and his maple empire continued long after his death. Cary's rise to prominence in the maple industry is not unknown to many in its general outline. Over the years authors have retold the tale in various forms such as in excellent articles by Lois Greer in 1929 and Sherb Doubleday in 1990, along with small section of the more recent books *Sweet Maple* by Lawrence and Martin, *Maple Sugaring in Vermont* by Betty Ann Lockhardt and *A Brief History of St. Johnsbury* by Peggy Pearl.[23] These works are all excellent introductions to the story of George Cary, but the literature was lacking a comprehensive narrative that looks at his life, his legacy, and the role his company played in the maple industry both during his lifetime and beyond. This book aims to fill that void and show the breadth of Cary's reach into nearly all segments of the maple world in the early twentieth century. For example, this account looks at how Cary became the Maple King and what life was like in his maple realm and court. Like all great empires it eventually failed, begging the question: what brought about its end and what became of the kingdom?

Figure 1.5: Postcard of Cary Maple Sugar Company plant on Portland Avenue in St. Johnsbury, ca. 1920-1928 (Author's Collection).

Largely organized in a chronological fashion this book recounts how maple sugar and syrup were good to George C. Cary and how he brought that to bear on his presence and place in and around St. Johnsbury. Through the installation of a modern and model sugarbushes and progressive farms in North Danville, the construction of an elegant home on Main Street, and the erection of a massive factory and processing complex on the edge of town (Figure 1.5), Cary was responsible for solidifying maple sugar in the identity of the St. Johnsbury community.

The Maple King's reign was not to last forever, and Cary's life ended abruptly on the heels of a catastrophic personal bankruptcy and company restructuring. These tragedies did not completely spell the end of the story for the Cary Maple Sugar Company and St. Johnsbury's claim to the title of Maple Capital of the World. How and why Cary's empire crumbled is examined in detail in Chapter Five as a pretext to what became of the Cary Company and the ongoing place of St. Johnsbury in the maple products marketplace. Following Cary's death, the bulk maple products industry witnessed something of a reshuffling of market shares, and the Cary Company and its subsidiaries would never again wield the control and influence of the first thirty years of the twentieth century. But as discussed in Chapter Six, under the wing of new leadership the Cary Company and Maple Grove continued to evolve and retain an important role in the larger maple products world. To appreciate the legacy of George Cary and recognize how the Cary Company arrived at its place in the world today we must first understand where the Cary Company came from and how it began many years before.

- MAPLE KING -

2

Formation of the Kingdom

The Birth of a King

George Clinton Cary's story begins with his birth on March 7, 1864 in the small town of Fort Fairfield, Maine near the Canadian border. George was the son of Asa Clinton Cary, a farmer and merchant, and Jessie Priestly Cary, a school teacher and later the Principal at the preparatory school connected to Colby College in Waterville, Maine. George attended public school in Fort Fairfield. He followed this with additional schooling at the Houlton Academy and at the Ricker Classical Institute in Houlton, Maine between 1882 and 1884. Shortly after graduating, Cary worked as a rural school teacher and sold farm machinery in the Fort Fairfield area. His teaching career was short-lived and at age 22 he entered the world of the "drummer" or traveling salesmen. For twelve years he was a traveling grocery salesman working by horse and buggy across northern New England. Initially he worked for Charles E. Jose & Company of Portland, Maine for one year. For the following three years, beginning in February 1886, he worked for the Twitchell, Champlin & Company out of Portland, Maine which regularly brought him to Vermont. In 1889 he began to work selling for Martin L. Hall out of Boston which lasted about one year before he left the grocery sales business and focused on buying and selling maple products and wood shingles full time.[24]

It wasn't long into his tenure as a traveling salesman with Twitchell Champlin & Company that the seeds of Cary's maple sugaring empire were sown, the story of which has been recounted numerous times in print. The story begins something like this. In April of 1886, while on his route selling groceries between Morrisville and Craftsbury, Vermont, Cary's team of horses was delayed by the thawing roads of the spring mud season. This forced him to spend the night in Craftsbury and wait for the ground to freeze before moving on the next morning (Figure 2.1).

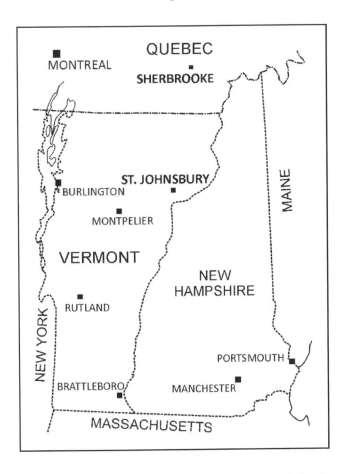

Figure 2.1: Map showing important locations in Vermont and Quebec.

- MAPLE KING -

On past sales visits through Craftsbury he had been unsuccessful in convincing the storekeeper to buy any of his groceries. However, with the time he had available that afternoon, due to his having to stay in town for the night, he didn't rush things and spent more time working on a sale with the storekeeper.

The storekeeper was resistant and still wasn't too keen on buying anything from Cary, but he did come up with a unique offer. If Cary would accept payment in maple sugar at four and a half cents a pound, the merchant would buy an order of Cary's groceries. The offer likely involved the previous year's sugar since it was April and local farmers would soon be trying to sell that year's maple crop. Eager to make a sale, Cary agreed to those terms and soon found himself with 1,500 pounds of maple sugar. Upon returning to Portland from his sales trip, the managers at Twitchell, Champlin & Company grocery firm were none too pleased and informed him that he was now responsible for getting rid of this sugar and turning it into real money.

Cary went away wondering how or where he was going to unload this sugar, but he didn't wonder for long. While traveling on a train later that spring he had the good fortune to meet a tobacco company salesman who was traveling through Maine. Through their conversation, Cary discovered that tobacco companies at the time used a great deal of Barbados cane sugar in processing and flavoring plug tobacco which they purchased at five cents a pound. He learned that the tobacco leaves were dipped in the sticky West Indies sugar and then pressed together. Cary asked the tobacco salesman if anyone had ever tried using maple sugar and if it would work the same way, to which the tobacco man replied, that he didn't see why it wouldn't. So, Cary offered to sell him all of his 1,500 pounds of maple sugar at four and a half cents a pound, a half a cent per pound less than the tobacco folks were paying for the cane sugar. The tobacco salesman replied that he couldn't make such a commitment for his company. Cary then offered to sell one hundred boxes of his plug tobacco in exchange if he would at least try the sugar, to which he agreed to take 200 pounds of the sugar in exchange.[25]

17

Thanks to this unknown risk-taking tobacco salesman, the Wright Tobacco Company of Richmond, Virginia received the shipment of 200 pounds of maple sugar and gave it a try on an experimental basis. Wright Tobacco seemed satisfied and soon after ordered all 1300 pounds of the maple sugar Cary still had on hand. From there, they decided they wanted to use maple sugar for processing all of their tobacco and Cary now found himself in the position of becoming a maple sugar broker. As a side business to his ongoing work as a drummer, Cary began actively seeking maple sugar to buy along his sales routes in Vermont.

Through the late 1880s Cary's work as a maple sugar broker continued to grow but he was still predominantly engaged selling groceries out of western Maine. In June of 1891 Cary married Teresa Burnham of Houlton, Maine and two years later in September, their daughter Teresa, known affectionately as "Little Trissie," was born. Tragically, three months later, Cary's wife Teresa contracted pneumonia and died in Houlton. Despite this loss, Cary continued to work as a drummer for Martin L. Hall and Company spending most of his days traveling from village to village on the roads of Vermont. In this capacity, Cary had traveled through and stayed in St. Johnsbury many times and had established numerous sales accounts in the area. Having developed a familiarity with and affection for the Northeast Kingdom, in 1895 he permanently relocated to St. Johnsbury. At that time, on behalf of his employer, Martin L. Hall and Co. of Boston, he established a wholesale grocery branch in the basement of the Citizen's block along Railroad Street in St. Johnsbury.[26]

Finding himself in the role of the single parent to a young child while holding a profession that took him away from home for most of his days, Cary likely moved his daughter to live with her grandmother and grandfather Burnham in Houlton. However, George suffered another devastating blow when soon after moving her to Maine, his young daughter Trissie passed away in Houlton in August of 1896 at the age of three.[27]

It is impossible to say if the stress and pain of losing one's child precipitated or exacerbated what was to come, but in the later months of 1896 Cary was involved in a bizarre fracas with another traveling salesman named J.G. Bussing. As the story goes, both men were traveling on a train and something in their conversation led Bussing to call Cary a liar, which Cary did not take kindly to and let Bussing know it by firmly grabbing Bussing by the neck. Bussing asserted that Cary grabbed him with such force that his vocal cords were permanently damaged, and therefore sued Cary for $10,000 in damages.[28] Bussing claimed to have previously been engaged in singing but was no longer able to enjoy this pastime due to the damage caused by George Cary. Cary and Bussing went to court to settle the matter in the spring of 1899. According to Cary's daughter Madeline Cary Fleming, Bussing was represented by Attorney Alex Dunnett, who when given the chance to cross-examine George Cary, asked Cary to explain what happened. Cary responded that he merely, "tapped the fellow lightly," to which Attorney Dunnett requested that Cary demonstrate. Cary obliged with a light punch toward Dunnett, who, in an exaggerated over-reaction and in a great show of acting, staggered backwards. In the end, Dunnett prevailed in the case for his client and Cary, being so impressed with his bravado, hired Dunnett to be his own personal attorney from that day forward.[29]

The loss of first his wife and then his daughter did not seem to deter a driven man like George Cary. If anything, he threw himself more aggressively into growing his business and reputation in St. Johnsbury. Cary was still on the road selling groceries but was also spending more and more time managing the Martin L. Hall and Co. wholesale branch as well as buying and selling maple sugar for his personal enterprise. In addition, Cary's business in the late 1800s and early 1900s also included a notable trade across New England of cedar and pine shingles. Most of the shingles he sold were milled in Maine and New Brunswick.

With an established traveling grocery business and growing maple sugar and shingle businesses, Cary needed a place to stable his fleet of horses. He also needed room to store and handle the maple syrup and sugar, along with access to the railroad for shipping. In October of 1897 he purchased a lot and erected a new horse stable adjacent to Henry Ide's grain elevator on Bay Street in St. Johnsbury, in what was known as Ide's Addition or Ide's Back Bay. In the spring of 1898 Cary expanded this structure by adding a storehouse to the property (Figure 2.2).[30] With the construction of his large warehouse on Bay Street next to Ide's Mill, Cary was able to take advantage of this warehouse being located immediately adjacent to the parallel lines of the Boston and Maine Railroad and the St. Johnsbury and Lake Champlain Railroad for convenient shipping of his products.[31]

Figure 2.2: Early 1900s photo of Cary building on Bay Street with Ide mill in background (Courtesy of Fairbanks Museum and Planetarium).

St. Johnsbury had proven to be an ideal location for the nineteenth century model of manufacturing, with many well-placed mill sites along the Passumpsic and Moose Rivers and abundant natural resources in reasonably close-proximity. But it was St. Johnsbury's access to the railroads, combined with the available industrial workforce, that Cary found inviting for taking his maple enterprise into the twentieth century.

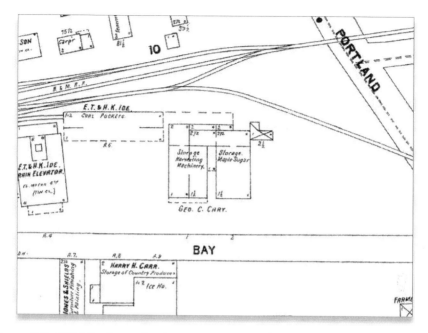

Figure 2.3: 1905 Sanborn fire insurance map of Bay Street businesses showing Cary building (Courtesy of Library of Congress.)

While St. Johnsbury became the new residence and business home of George Cary, his connections to Maine were clearly not severed and in May of 1898 he married Annie Mae Partridge in Skowhegan, Maine. Following a short honeymoon in New England, they settled into a house on the corner of Main and Mt. Pleasant Streets in St. Johnsbury to start a family. The following March, their son Clinton P. Cary was born followed by daughter Madeline J. Cary a few years later in November of 1901. Their third and final child, daughter Ruth E. Cary, was born in May 1909. By the end of 1899, the maple sugar portion of Cary's business had grown to such a degree that he opted to focus on maple sugar full-time and discontinued selling groceries and wood shingles. From that time forward Cary's work was exclusively focused on the Cary Maple Sugar Company.

Crowning of a King

The buying of maple sugar and maple syrup for repacking and selling, a job that has sometimes been referred to as a "packer," went so well for Cary at the beginning of the new century that he began to establish a series of warehouses along railroad lines around Vermont. At these warehouses, representatives for the Cary Maple Sugar Company would accept sugar and syrup for purchase and delivery and store their products prior to being shipped by rail to their processing plant on Bay Street in St. Johnsbury (Figure 2.3). They accepted sugar for purchase at these warehouses at any time during the year. For example, in the town of Morrisville, Cary erected a 30 by 40 foot warehouse adjacent to the railroad line.[32] Cary normally sold and shipped his maple sugar in wooden crates, especially to the tobacco firms, but in 1902 he reported that his company made a shipment of maple sugar in metal tins, sent by rail car to a customer in Detroit, Michigan.[33]

Filling these many warehouses with sugar and syrup was made possible by the Cary Company contracting hundreds of local buyers to work on their behalf, purchasing maple products from farmers in their local area or territories. Buyers signed a yearly contract to work exclusively with the Cary Company, whereby they were advanced cash to purchase sugar and syrup and agreed to deliver it to their local Cary Company warehouse. In exchange for their efforts, they received a commission on what they bought for the company. For example, Figure 2.4 shows a 1907 contract between T.W. Hale of Fairfield, Vermont and the Cary Company. The contract, signed by John Rickaby, dictated Hale was to receive a quarter cent commission on all the maple sugar and a three-cent commission on the maple syrup he purchased.[34]

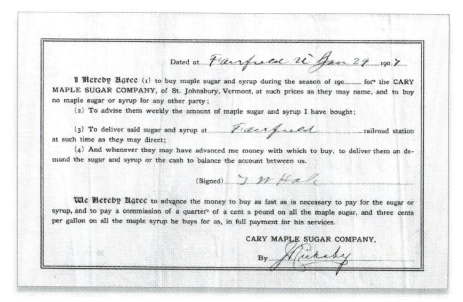

Figure 2.4: 1907 buyers contract (Author's Collection).

From very early on in his sugar buying business, Cary engaged not only in buying maple sugar from Vermont and New England sugarmakers, but also from Canadian producers, primarily from Quebec. A 1906 advertisement is clear in declaring the Cary Maple Sugar Company as wholesale dealers in Vermont and Canadian maple sugar (Figure 2.5).[35] The bulk of the sugar and syrup purchased by Cary in these early years was processed and sold to tobacco firms, mostly in Virginia. Cary also sold sugar for blending and flavoring. An early blending customer of the Cary Company was Towle's Log Cabin Syrup who made syrup blended from approximately 50 percent maple sugar and 50 percent cane sugar.[36] The Towle's connection would continue to grow and deepen over the following decade as discussed in Chapter Three.

As early as 1900, Cary's maple products business was described as covering a quarter of a million dollars in revenue.[37] By October first of 1901 Cary reported that he had sold about 900,000 pounds of maple sugar that year. This report resulted in a remark by the St. Johnsbury

Caledonian newspaper that such extensive dealings in the product had earned Cary the title "Maple Sugar King", and thus the Maple King was crowned.[38] This may have been the earliest comment in print assigning that title and throne to Cary's name. The appropriateness of this title would only grow in the coming years.

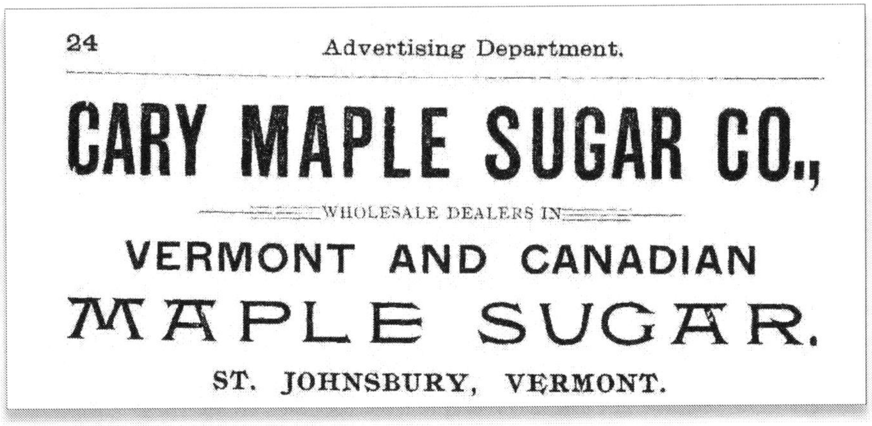

> **24**   Advertising Department.
>
> # CARY MAPLE SUGAR CO.,
> ===WHOLESALE DEALERS IN===
> ## VERMONT AND CANADIAN
> # MAPLE SUGAR.
> ST. JOHNSBURY, VERMONT.

Figure 2.5: 1906 St. Johnsbury directory advertisement (Chronicling America website).

With such rapid growth, George Cary was ready to take his little maple sugar company to the next level, and in December 1904 the Cary Maple Sugar Company was formally incorporated with $125,000 of capital investment. The first Board of Directors consisted of George Cary as general manager, Edward McLellan of Boston as President, Fred Peaslee Virgin of Boston as Vice President, Charles G. Burgess of Boston as Treasurer, along with John L. Lewis of North Troy, Vermont; G.M. Campbell of Lyndonville, and W.A. Ricker of St. Johnsbury as members at large.[39] Fred Peaslee Virgin served as the Company's first Vice President until his death in 1908. Virgin and George Cary had worked together for several years as traveling salesmen for the Boston wholesale grocers Martin L. Hall & Company.[40] Following Virgin's death, John Rickaby, previously one of Cary's first sugar buyers, served as company Vice President until Rickaby took the position as plant manager for the Towle's Maple Products Company in 1910. With his departure to Towle's, Rickaby was replaced by G.M. Campbell as the Cary Company's Vice President.[41]

The Royal Family
Like any good businessman and leading citizen in a town, from early on Cary was very active in various social and commercial groups and local as well as national boards of directors, including the Board for the Towle's Maple Products Company out of St. Paul, Minnesota, the makers of Log Cabin Syrup. He was also very active on the Board of Directors of the Passumpsic Telephone Company, occasionally speaking on their behalf and answering the rate payer's questions. For many years he was the President of the Caledonia County Fair and was a member of the Eastern Frontier Lodge of the Freemasons and the Fort Fairfield Lodge of the Independent Order of the Odd Fellows. In 1917 he became the President of the St. Johnsbury Commercial Club, a role that would come into play a few years later with his plans for building a large plant on east Portland Street (see Chapter Three). Cary was always a member of the Republican Party and for many years served as a local delegate to the State convention. The Cary family attended the Congregationalist Church.[42]

During World War I, Cary was frequently at the helm of campaigns to sell and buy Liberty Bonds supporting the war effort, no doubt a sentiment fueled by the fact that his son Clinton was serving overseas. Leading up to and during the years of World War I, Cary was an outspoken supporter of assistance groups and the federal government. In 1917 he was a featured speaker at an event aimed at rousing the patriotic energies of the people of St. Johnsbury. At this event Cary and his colleagues warned that, "this war is to be a real war" and specifically asked the audience to support the Red Cross and their government and begin to make changes to their way of living which might assist the war effort.[43]

Cary contracted scarlet fever in his childhood which resulted in his suffering from progressive loss of his hearing. By his twenties his hearing loss became more and more noticeable and by his thirties he was forced to use a trumpet-style hearing aid. By 1910, at age 46, Cary had become completely deaf. Cary was generally able to read lips and always had a pad and pencil in his pocket. However, it is clear from the report of his public address in 1917, that his ability to speak remained strong. By this time, he never traveled out of Vermont alone, and instead preferred the accompaniment of one of his children or his personal secretary, Gertrude Franklin. Cary did not necessarily view his deafness as a liability; in fact, he often put it to good use in his business dealings by being able to avoid the usual chit-chat about the weather and other social niceties that frequently began a conversation.

Figure 2.6: Side by side photos of George C Cary and Annie Mae Cary in fur coats (Courtesy Cary Family Archives).

Not surprisingly, Cary was a fan of silent movies, especially Charlie Chaplin films, a fact that may have played into his later efforts at creating a silent film depicting the history of maple sugaring and his sugar and syrup packing business.[44]

Among men of his time, Cary might have been described as of a solid build. He stood around six feet tall and weighed in at 210 pounds (Figure 2.6). His size and stature even qualified him for membership in St. Johnsbury's branch of the New England Fat Men's Club, a social organization for men tipping the scales at 200 pounds or more.[45] A Boston Post reporter even went so far as to compare Cary and his physical build to Cary's beloved oxen, due to his "sturdy patience that has kept right on the job through all difficulties".[46]

Cary took to the automobile very quickly and was one of the first to own such a vehicle in St. Johnsbury. Unfortunately for Cary, in the early twentieth century the rural roads around St. Johnsbury and nearby North Danville were not yet designed and built for motor vehicle travel, especially during the spring thaws. Cary was constantly needing a pull from a team of horses to extract him from the mud. It seems that Cary also had a habit of driving a little quickly for the conditions, which, combined with his deafness, made for several collisions with him at the wheel. Cary's daughter Madeline Cary Fleming recalled that their first automobile arrived around 1906 and was a two-cylinder Brush, which was followed by a 1908 Buick, a Packard, a Stearns-Knight in 1913, and ultimately a Cadillac.[47]

Annie Mae Cary, like her husband, was not afraid to tackle community affairs and found much work to do with the social causes and organizations of St. Johnsbury. She was an active member and leader of the Woman's Club, the Suffrage Study Group, the Women's Auxiliary of the American Legion, the Girls Community League, the Hospital Association, the school board, the North Congregational Church, and the Republican State Committee, just to name a few. She led numerous Red Cross drives for the war effort during World War I, was an officer for the summertime Chautauqua events, and promoted many educational improvements in the St. Johnsbury area. The Carys frequently hosted musical recitals in their home and welcomed these social groups to gather at their rural Pine Lodge property.[48]

Clinton P. Cary, known familiarly as Clint, was the only son of George and Annie Mae Cary and would grow up to advance into a position of assistant manager in the Cary Company and eventually become Vice President of Maple Grove Candies. His initial school years were spent at the St. Johnsbury Academy, for his junior and senior years of secondary school he attended the St. Luke's School, a boy's boarding school in Wayne, Pennsylvania.[49]

Clinton Cary enlisted in 1918 and was assigned to the United States Army Coast Artillery Corps where he was sent to France and stationed near Limoges. He never saw action because the armistice was signed the same day his unit was preparing to be called into action. Clinton returned to the States and resumed his studies at Dartmouth, graduated in 1921, after which he immediately began work with his father's company. Clinton spent a few years learning the business and working his way through various parts of the company before advancing to become a sugar and syrup buyer and member of the board of directors.[50]

A hint of Clinton Cary's future as a businessman was demonstrated at an early age when he and his friend Kenneth Flint ventured into the milk delivery business. Clinton was only eight years old at the time and Kenneth was eleven years old when the two began to bring fresh milk to town from the family's Pine Lodge farm in large milk cans on a wagon drawn by Shetland ponies. The milk was ladled into the quart cans of their waiting customers. These two entrepreneurs even had invoices made up with the titles Cary and Flint, Milk Merchants.

Clinton and Kenneth taught a pair of George's two-year-old Devon steers to perform a series of stunts and tricks which the boys presented at a few local fairs for a small admittance fee, including an exhibition in Red Bank, New Jersey.[51]

George Cary's daughters, Madeline and Ruth, both attended school at the St. Johnsbury Academy like their older brother. Madeline went on to attend the Mary Lyons School in Swarthmore, Pennsylvania, before completing her college studies at Smith College (Figure 2.7). Madeline was better known by the nickname "Sue" and following college married Maurice Flemming but never had any children.

Figure 2.7: Clinton Cary, Ruth Cary, and Madeline Cary, L to R (Courtesy of the Cary Family Archives).

Following graduation from the St. Johnsbury Academy, Ruth went to work in the St. Johnsbury and New York City offices of the Cary Company for several years in the late 1920s and early 1930s before marrying Stephen Aldrich, another graduate of St. Johnsbury Academy. Ruth and Stephen had two daughters named Nancy Cary Aldrich and Mary Louise Aldrich.

The daughters of Ruth Cary recall hearing their mother tell of her and her sister's years as children and spending time at the family farm in North Danville. Both Madeline and Ruth were fond of riding their horses and ponies far out onto the farm, but it was Madeline who was a serious competitive rider, bringing home the occasional ribbon for her efforts.[52] Being the children of a prominent and relatively wealthy man in the town of St. Johnsbury, the Cary daughters were expected to behave accordingly. The task of teaching such behavior was assigned to George's secretary, Gertrude Franklin, who taught them the appropriate social graces for young women in a nouveau-riche family. Additionally, the Cary household had a housekeeper who may also have served as a sort of nanny or governess.

Building a Palace in Town
As would be fitting for any newly crowned Maple Sugar King, Cary established a lasting physical presence in St. Johnsbury. In February 1901 Cary purchased a small lot on the west side of Main Street from Henry Fairbanks for $1,750. Located between the houses of Ephraim Jewett (P.D. Blodgett) and D.D. Patterson, the lot was only four rods wide (66 feet), which was an unbelievably narrow lot in comparison to other nearby lots on the affluent stretch of Main Street known locally as "The Plain".

Figure 2.8: Modern photo of Cary home on corner of Cary Place and Main Street (photo by author).

At the time of this sale a right-of-way for a short dead-end road was established on the north side of the lot, which was later named Cary

Place.⁵³ As it was one of the more recently built homes among mansions and Victorian homes along Main Street, the Cary the outside appears practically modest. Its monochromatic white exterior paint scheme is in muted contrast to the vibrant colors of the "painted ladies" found among its neighbors on Main Street (Figure 2.8).

Prior to the home Cary built in 1901 on Main Street, the Cary family's first residence in St. Johnsbury was an existing house at the corner of Main and Mt. Pleasant Streets. This home was sold by Cary in 1899 to E.M. Taft, a state legislator from Peacham, Vermont for $8000. With the sale of the home on Main and Pleasant, the Carys promptly moved into the former home of Mrs. Fred Carpenter on Webster Street and soon after began proceedings to establish their new abovementioned home at what was then known as 96 ½ Main Street.⁵⁴

A.D. Houghton, a well-known architect and engineer frequently employed by John D. Rockefeller, was commissioned to design the house for Cary. Construction of the home was completed in 1902 under the direction of James Foye.⁵⁵ The new Cary home was built with a fully cemented cellar containing a laundry and an oil burning boiler for heating the entire house. The rooms upstairs all featured hardwood floors and elaborate trim finished in birch and oak. There were three fireplaces and two full bathrooms on the upper floors along with a smaller bathroom on the ground floor.

Originally designated with the house number 96 1/2 Main Street, in the 1920s the numbering system for Main Street was modified slightly, shifting numbers up two, four, or six places, resulting in the Cary house being renumbered 102 Main Street, the number assigned to it to this day (Figure 2.9).

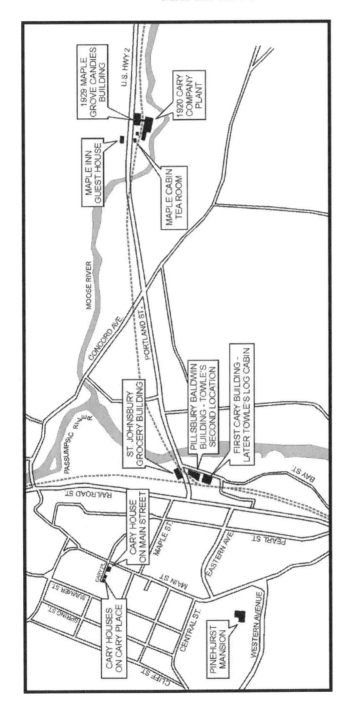

Figure 2:9: Map showing locations of important places in St. Johnsbury.

Cary was not satisfied with just the one beautiful home on Main Street. In 1909 he had a short, one block long street installed adjacent to the north side of his home, dead-ending at the back of his lot. Naming the street "Cary Place", he had two additional homes built on this street, one in 1909 and one in 1910. These homes were used as rental properties and at different periods as private residences for his children and some of his closest staff. These were sold by Cary in 1921 and remain separate residential properties.

Conquering Lands in the Countryside

Along with embedding himself and his family in the physical and social structure of St. Johnsbury, Cary also asserted his presence and began to claim a domain in the townships of rural Caledonia County.

Lookout Farm

North Danville became a fixture in George Cary's life when, in 1898, he purchased land that he referred to as Lookout Farm (Figure 2.13). With Lookout Farm, Cary was in the beginning stages of his life as a sort of gentleman farmer, in which his primary home was in town and his full-time business was as a merchant (Figure 2.10). To successfully manage and operate such properties from "afar", Cary employed a collection of different farmers or caretakers and housed them on site. Lookout Farm was not just for raising stock. Cary also operated a sugarbush at the farm, making syrup and sugar himself each spring in the sugarhouse. Sugaring activities at the Lookout Farm sugarbush were even featured in a series of photos in a small informational and promotional booklet put out by the Cary Company in the early part of the 1900s. In one photo, George Cary is shown working a team of oxen pulling a sap-gathering tank on a sled with the sugarhouse in the background.

Owning woodlands in the North Danville area allowed Cary to engage in making maple sugar and syrup in his own sugarbush. How much time Cary spent in the sugarbush during the tapping and boiling season is not exactly clear, but we do know that he did get into the woods to drive his oxen and at least supervise the springtime work.

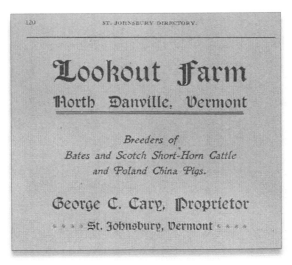

Figure 2.10: Advertisement for Lookout Farm from 1901 St. Johnsbury directory (Chronicling America website).

With the purchase of Lookout Farm, Cary began his foray into using the resources from his commercial maple sugar business to develop a modern, model farm. Lookout Farm was equipped with a telephone connection and other up-to-date amenities. In fact, beyond simply having a private line installed to his Lookout Farm, in the fall of 1901 Cary arranged for the installation of a "farmer's line," a local privately-owned telephone exchange, connecting many farms in the North Danville area.[56]

In July 1901 The Lookout Farm survived a tragic lightning strike to the farm's largest barn. The resulting fire burned the barn to the ground and fourteen cows, eight calves and one sheep inside were killed. Seven other prized cattle were also killed at the farm in the same storm when lightning struck the tree they were standing under. Among those killed were an imported cow named Gladys, valued at $750. Cary wisely carried $7,500 worth of insurance on his farm against such loss and was able to recover $4330 from his insurance company.[57] In the summer of 1902,

Cary replenished a large portion of this herd with a shipment of 28 Shorthorn cows and bulls from breeders in Ontario.[58]

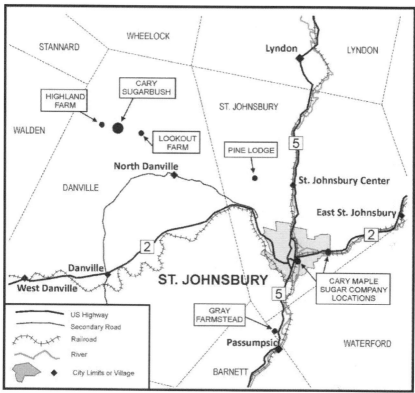

Figure 2.11: Map of important locations in Caledonia County.

Lookout Farm as a holding in the Cary Kingdom was short-lived and Cary decided to sell Lookout Farm and put his energies toward acquiring and improving additional properties in North Danville. Cary had an auction in September 1903 to reduce or eliminate his Lookout Farm stock. Held at the fairgrounds in St. Johnsbury, it was advertised that for sale were Poland China hogs and registered Shorthorn cattle that were part of a larger herd that "was probably the best and largest of American Short horn cattle in the East".[59]

Pine Lodge

Lookout Farm, in the amount of 300 acres, was sold in the summer of 1903. Around the same time Cary purchased the Aldrich Farm near an area that is commonly known as "Four Corners" in Caledonia County, a mere two miles from St. Johnsbury. Cary purchased the Aldrich property with the intention of building a barn and summer cottage for his family from which he could easily travel back and forth each day, rather than endure the longer trip to his Lookout Farm which was farther up in the hills of North Danville. Cary was a man who usually worked rather late at the office and he welcomed a shorter trip home by horse and buggy each summer night. Cary wasted no time developing the property he would name Pine Lodge and began construction on a barn in July 1902 and completed the cottage the following summer.[60]

Cary's daughter Madeline recalled that Pine Lodge was run under the watchful eye of a "faithful Scotsman" named John McBain. Curiously, this small farm was configured such that all the wagons and carriages and other vehicles of the farm were of a smaller size to be pulled by any number of the 60 Welsh ponies kept on site, essentially running the farm by "pony power."[61] Sadly for Annie Mae Cary, summer hay fever was a common concern at Pine Lodge and in later years she took to spending the summer at the summer cottage of her parents, Joseph and Emma Partridge, in Pemaquid Beach, Maine.

In 1899, Cary continued to expand his farm holdings in North Danville beyond Lookout Farm with his purchase of the Jonathan Batchelder Farm located along what is today Tampico Road. Purchased for a price of $3,500, this farm was well regarded at the time as one of the finest properties in the county.[62] In September of 1900, Cary added another 200 acres with the purchase of a property known as the George Drew Farm located to the east of the Batchelder Farm along Stanton Road.[63] However, just one short year later, it was reported that Cary had sold the Drew Farm.[64] Cary was certainly coming into his own as a buyer and seller of property, both in St. Johnsbury and in the fields and woods of North Danville.

Highland Farm

Cary's presence as a landowner in North Danville was solidified with the acquisition of the G. W. Sprague Farm a few miles northwest of the Batchelder and Drew farms. Situated in the northwestern corner of Caledonia County, the G.W. Sprague Farm included a complex of buildings and large barns with expansive open fields and boasted commanding views to the south and east. The farm sported many hundreds of acres of large, open fields with maple covered hills rising behind to the west and north. At the time of purchase, this farm was owned and operated by the Sprague family and was known by the name of Mapledale. Mapledale was unquestionably one of the finest farms in the county and was featured with an engraving depicting the house and main barn in the F.W. Beers 1875 Atlas of Caledonia County (Figure 2.12).[65] Under Cary's ownership, this farm served as the core of what Cary renamed Highland Farm.

Figure 2.12: Mapledale Farm from Beers 1875 Atlas (Courtesy of Fairbanks Museum and Planetarium).

In 1914 Cary expanded his holdings at Highland Farm to enlarge the sugarbush along the wooded ridge to the east of the fields of the old Sprague Farm. Cary bought the farm of A.C. Stanton which included an existing sugarbush and sugarhouse that was built in 1910.[66] As shown in Figure 2.13, Cary was never one to miss an advertising opportunity. This sugarhouse was painted barn-red, had cedar shakes for siding, and had the words "Cary Maple Sugar Company" painted in white letters on the side. Facing east where the base of the maple ridge meets the edge of a field, it was a perfect location for gathering sap via a gravity fed system such as the Brower Pipeline System, which Cary used extensively in this location.

Adjacent and to the north of the Stanton sugarbush was the sugarbush of the Stephen Waterman family, which Cary also purchased in 1914. Stephen Waterman originally purchased the sugarbush in 1904 as part of the acreage associated with a large, elegant farm and home known then as Grouselands. This farm, and the above-mentioned Sprague's Mapledale Farm, were the only two farms from North Danville featured in the 1875 F.W. Beers Illustrated County Atlas of Caledonia County.[67]

Soon after his 1914 purchase of the Waterman sugarbush, Cary built a new sugarhouse on the site, reportedly using timber that was recycled when the old grist mill was torn down in North Danville in 1913. Cary purchased the lumber specifically to be used to construct the new sugar house at his Highland Farm.[68] Located towards the middle of the sugarbush and down a forest road west of the main Waterman family farmstead, this was a very large sugarhouse with tongue-and-groove siding, and, like its neighbor, the old Stanton sugarhouse, was painted barn red with white trim around the doors, windows, and cornice. As evident in Figure 2.19, prominent along the east wall of the sugarhouse and painted in large letters were the words "Cary Maple Sugar Co.". This was what might be described as one of Cary's showpiece sugarhouses, and as a result it too appeared in the 1927 silent film.

The Waterman family renamed the Grouselands farmhouse to its current name of Broadview Farm when they purchased it in 1904 and have continued to retain ownership of these buildings ever since. George Cary only purchased their sugarbush and never the Grouselands/Broadview Farm house and barns. The main buildings of the farm are a complex of connected house, service wing, and wagon shed. It was built in 1865 in an Italianate style but modified in 1904 to a Shingle style with Colonial Revival elements. The historic significance of the property was easily-recognized, and Grouselands/Broadview Farm was listed on the National Register of Historic Places in 1983. However, this nomination was limited to the buildings and features in the immediate vicinity of the house complex and did not include the Cary sugarhouse located a short distance away.[69]

Figure 2.13: Stanton sugarhouse under Cary ownership (Courtesy of Vermont Historical Society).

Figure 2.14: Waterman Farm sugarhouse under Cary ownership (Courtesy of Tom Olson and New England Maple Museum).

Cary maintained a wide variety of stock at his North Danville farms which he often displayed at public events such as parades and at state and county fairs. Many of his animals were considered high-end breeding stock and were regularly entered in judged competitions. More than a few blue ribbons and grand champion trophies were awarded to George Cary. Between 1915 and 1920 at the Caledonia County Fair, Cary entered a dozen or more Bates and Scotch Shorthorn cattle from his Pine Lodge Farm, led by his bull of the name "Castleton Hero." Cary displayed nearly a dozen Herefords from his Highland Farm, including a two-year old cow he purchased for over $800, an extremely high price for a female Hereford at the time. In addition to Herefords and Shorthorn cattle, Cary was known to show Holsteins, Devons, and Guernsey, as well as steer and oxen.[70]

In his earlier years of stock raising, Cary was particularly known for raising Welsh ponies as well as for raising and racing horses. Occasionally in the summer evenings Cary was found at the racetrack in

Newport cheering on his race horses. Sometimes he won, but more often than not, he lost and eventually discontinued his interest in horse racing.[71]

If it is any indication of the seriousness with which Cary approached cattle breeding and competition, The American Hereford Journal wrote in 1919 that Cary "frequently has shown two and three breeds of cattle at one fair. His reputation is that of a good loser but one who makes his competitors come back the next time with something better if they want to stay with him."[72] Cary's main venue for showing his stock in competition was the Caledonia County Fair, but he also regularly brought a smaller menagerie of animals to the Vermont State Fair in White River Junction. In 1911 he traveled to Chicago with three milking cows, one steer and three ponies to show at the International Livestock Show, where some of his stock were awarded first place ribbons.[73] Cary did not limit himself to raising purebred cattle and was also proud of his draft horses and saddle horses. From his Pine Lodge Farm, he also regularly brought to the fair a fine collection of Poland China swine, he raised sheep as well.

Perhaps Cary's greatest love in the stock raising arena was driving oxen. Cary was a regular supporter and participant in the horse versus oxen pulls at the fair in which his oxen usually won. Cary is shown in numerous photographs working a team of oxen in his North Danville sugarbushes.

George Cary's interest in raising and showing stock carried over to his support for and leadership in promoting and organizing the Caledonia County Fair. Upon his relocation to St. Johnsbury from Maine and his becoming a landowning resident of Caledonia County he quickly became a regular fixture in the county fair's stock pavilions. In later years he expanded his involvement and became the county fair president, leading the planning for each summer's events and lending his considerable influence and assertive business style to fundraising efforts. In 1919, under Cary's term as fair president, a record 12,000 attended the Caledonia County Fair in a single day.[74]

Having many acres of forest to manage on his North Danville land holdings, Cary incorporated the Highland Lumber Company in 1914 to facilitate logging operations in the woodlands of his Highland Farm.[75] At the Highland Farm, Cary's sugaring operation grew to a point where his crews were tapping as many as 20,000 trees and feeding the sap to half a dozen sugarhouses. Initially, the sap gathering was done entirely with covered pails, but by the early 1920s, Cary had converted much of his sugarbush to the Brower pipeline system (see Chapter Four for more discussion on the Brower Pipeline). Beyond the two prominent sugarhouses discussed above, Cary operated several other smaller sugarhouses in the maple woods around Highland Farm.[76]

In addition to the farm and sugarbush, Cary built a rustic retreat or Camp in the woodlands to the northwest of the Highland Farm. At times Cary would take his friends or children out to the camp for a more primitive outdoor experience.[77] The area of this rustic retreat was also the location of one of Cary's North Danville sugarbushes and sugarhouses.

Success in the maple business did not happen overnight for George Cary. That Cary came into the world of maple sugar and syrup with the experiences of a merchant and businessman and not that of a sugarmaker was probably to his advantage. Not limited in thinking by the conventional approach to the maple industry at the time, Cary was instead inspired and informed by a more business-minded approach to the sales and marketing of maple sugar. At least initially, Cary was not specifically concerned with improving the production-end of the maple industry. Instead, he left that to the creative minds of New England farmers, who continued to envision and apply technological improvements each year. Rather, he turned his attention to a less well-developed corner of the industry; namely, how to develop, open, and grow new markets for maple sugar and maple syrup in a time of changing consumer tastes and greater access to transportation infrastructure.

With a growing business and a growing family, Cary's role and prominence in the village of St. Johnsbury expanded to match his grandiose title, solidifying his name in the history books. A warehouse and processing facility was erected adjacent to the rail lines on Bay Street and an elegant residence was one of the last Main Street homes to be built among the residences of St. Johnsbury's other prominent businessmen and leading citizens.

The footprint of Cary's factory buildings continued to grow and were well-known and prominently on display in the village of St. Johnsbury. Far fewer were aware of his sugarbush complex in North Danville or know that he was once one of the largest landowners in Caledonia County. And while Cary made his living as a sugar merchant and maple producer, his success in these endeavors allowed him to continue to dabble in raising prized stock animals, which was arguably his first and true farm passion. Cary's footprint wasn't just within the village of St. Johnsbury; he also had a notable presence in the countryside of Caledonia County with his various retreats and farms and his consolidation and improvements to the large sugarbush at Highland Farm.

Without question, Cary's new maple sugar company was a success that would expand in size and scope, not just within St. Johnsbury, but across New England and adjacent Ontario and Quebec, to encompass and influence the entire maple sugar industry.

- MAPLE KING -

3

Expansion of the Kingdom

Through risks and ingenuity Cary brought a business sense and approach not previously witnessed in the maple industry. Before Cary, most maple producers were small scale farmers selling or trading their best products direct to the local consumer or to a local merchant or grocer. Cary approached the industry from another direction, applying economies of scale and using technology to expand and modernize sugaring. He bought more and more maple sugar and syrup at greater and greater volumes, moving it over much longer distances with the use of railroads, and processing it in industrial settings and at industrial volumes. The rewards were self-evident, and the Cary Company was a catalyst in the evolution of the bulk maple sugar and syrup market. Cary's growing financial strength permitted him to diversify his interests and enter into partnerships with other growing maple enterprises, notably the Towle's Maple Products Company and Maple Grove Candies. With a growing stronghold on the maple products market, Cary was able to dictate not only prices for maple sugar and syrup but also institute changes in the way maple products were prepared and delivered to him.

Working with the Sugarmakers

Expanding upon his initial experience selling maple sugar to the tobacco industry, Cary created a market for lower grades of bulk maple sugar and employed a team of traveling buyers and local buying ...atives complete with a network of warehouses on rail lines a... e northeastern United States. In the company's early years Cary purchased both sugar and syrup but over time shifted to only accept maple syrup purchased by the pound. Cary introduced the use of 55-gallon metal barrels or drums and had them delivered to the producers as a way to more efficiently move the product. Providing barrels to the producers also served as a kind of informal contract to ensure a degree of loyalty in the following spring when it was time for the producers to sell their syrup. The Cary Company then reprocessed the bulk syrup into seventy-pound blocks of solid maple sugar of a uniform consistency and quality. These solid blocks of sugar were easier to ship and use by the tobacco industry and other clients that were using maple sugar for flavoring.

Unlike other sugar buyers and packers, with the incorporation of the Cary Company in 1904 and a growing tobacco clientele, Cary had the capital and organization to offer producers a market for the harder to sell, but easier to make, lower grades of sugar and syrup. Initially, the Cary Company operated warehouses and collection points in Newport, Lyndonville, Greensboro and Morrisville, Vermont. By April of 1905 the company had erected warehouses across Vermont in Lyndonville, Barton, Newport, Richford, East Fairfield, Morrisville, Greensboro, Plainfield, West Burke, Barton Landing, North Troy, Enosburg Falls, Cambridge Junction and Hardwick, as well as Beauceville and Sherbrooke in Quebec.[78] However, his main center of operation continued to be the Bay Street warehouse and processing facility in St. Johnsbury. One of Cary's strengths was that his buyers went into the communities where the producers lived and collected the sugar and syrup at local depots, eliminating the costly need for the producers to travel great distances from their rural farms to the cities, like St. Johnsbury and Burlington, to try and sell their products. Producers appreciated this convenience, at least initially.

As examples of how significant Cary's buying power was, for t[he] season, the maple syrup makers in the Canton, New York area contracted the sale of their entire syrup crop for the year to the Cary Company for 80 cents a gallon.[79] Similarly, in 1910 sugarmakers in the Rochester, Vermont area sold the Cary Company half of the 500,000 pounds of maple sugar they produced. Such large scale buying and selling of sugar was facilitated by Cary's employment of a local Rochester based sales agent, Henry H. Cushman.[80]

The Cary Company was increasing its purchases of large quantities of maple sugar out of Canada, primarily from the Beauce region of Quebec. Not surprisingly, the sugar from this region was commonly referred to as "Beauce sugar" and was generally darker and stronger in flavor, making it preferable for use in blending and flavoring tobacco and other products.[81] At that time, the Beauce region had a long history of being the leading maple sugar producer in Canada, and yet, as much as two-thirds of the Beauce region's sugar production was being sold to the Cary Company.[82]

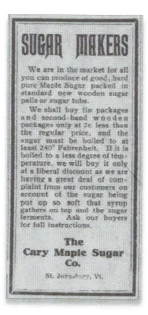

Figure 3.1: 1912 Notice to sugarmakers (Chronicling America website).

It was not uncommon into the 1910s for Cary to put out ads soliciting farmers to sell to the Cary Company all of their hard, pure maple sugar packed in wooden sugar pails or sugar tubs (Figure 3.1). In some cases, the sugar was packed in barrels that originally contained cane sugar or flour. Such ads also informed farmers that they would receive a noticeably lower price for inferior quality sugar and sugar packed in tins and used wooden containers.[83] Clearly, fresh, new wooden packing crates were preferred.

Much of the sugar purchased and sold at this time would be considered rather moist by today's refined sugar standards. Maple sugar in the early 1900s was nowhere near the dry, granulated, sand-like refined cane sugar people are accustomed to today. In many cases this maple sugar was downright wet and was poured into storage and shipping containers like a warm, thick cake batter that later cooled and solidified. However, unless the sugar was boiled to a higher temperature before packing, with cooling and settling, much of the remaining liquid in the sugar would seep out of the bottom of the containers. Sugar purchased from New England producers was a bit softer and wetter and was packed in a variety of containers. In contrast, Beauce sugar from Quebec tended to be drier and harder and came in smaller blocks, chunks, or cakes and was sometimes delivered in burlap sacks.

Unfortunately, these tubs, crates, and barrels of sugar too often contained more than maple sugar. Upon repacking the sugar that they had purchased by weight, workers at the Cary Company on occasion would find stones or bricks or wood or even sand at the bottom of the tub or barrel. In other cases, inferior quality sugar would be packed in the container and then topped off with a higher quality sugar, giving it the appearance of a full container of higher quality sugar. In one case, the Cary Company reported being sold a 35-pound tub filled with "a thin layer of sugar on top weighing about four pounds. This rested on a smaller tub cover and under it was two bricks, some smaller pieces of wood and rags and over 20 pounds in gravel."[84]

- MAPLE KING -

The Cary Company eventually tired of dealing with buying sugar laced with unseen foreign materials and inferior quality sugar being passed off as something better and began to move towards only buying liquid maple syrup in barrels which the company then boiled down to sugar and packed into their own uniform crates for shipment. It was the only effective way to ensure the quality of the product they were buying and selling. Adding additional quality controls to the buying process, in 1916 the Cary Company began buying 55-gallon steel drums to provide to the maple producers to fill with the syrup they intended to sell to Company.[85] The idea of storing and shipping maple syrup in 55-gallon steel drums may not have been invented exclusively by the Cary Company; however, it was not common before 1916. Their control of the maple sugar and syrup market was so great that through their influence and demand, use of barrels and buying and selling syrup by the pound became the industry standard. In many ways, maple producers liked it too since it used less time and fewer resources to boil maple sap down to syrup instead of sugar.

Cary continued to push the transition from buying sugar to buying only syrup from American producers. In a December 1st 1919 letter the Cary Company informed their sugar buyers that they would "not pay for packages in which sugar is packed this season as we will have to re-melt practically all of the tub sugar and packages have to be destroyed and cannot be used again." With their requirements for syrup, the company provided their barrels at no cost to the farmers. Cary noted "if any other concern will offer more for the syrup than we are paying, we will either meet the price or sell our barrels to the farmers at what they cost us and let them sell the syrup to the other parties."[86] Moving forward to 1921, the Cary Company further advised their buyers to purchase syrup rather than sugar and that "there is practically no demand for Vermont pail sugar and all we are now buying we are remelting and putting into cake form."[87]

By the late 1920s, the company itself owned nearly 50,000 metal barrels. Even then, there were seasons, such as 1929, in which there were not enough barrels available and producers were forced to ship drums to the plants where they were emptied and returned to the producer to be filled again.[88] With the Cary Company's shift away from buying maple sugar to buying liquid maple syrup, the production of maple sugar in the United States continued its decline and dwindled to nearly nothing by the 1920s. Maple sugar has never again been produced in any appreciable amounts, with the exception of the war time years when white table sugar was difficult to acquire and more expensive to purchase.

Figure 3.2: Block sugar drying in Cary warehouse (Courtesy Vermont Historical Society).

As recounted by Sherb Doubleday, the conversion of maple syrup to blocks of maple sugar had both advantages and disadvantages (Figure 3.2). On the one hand, the handling of standardized, seventy-pound blocks of sugar resulted in greater quality control and blending as well as shipping at a reduced weight and using less space than liquid syrup. By converting everything going out of the plant to block sugar, the many barrels used for transporting incoming syrup could also be emptied and readily re-used. However, reducing great volumes of syrup down to sugar with only seven percent water content and ninety-three percent solids removed many thousands of gallons of water and required a significant amount of heat and fuel. In addition, concerns with levels of invert sugars in darker maple syrup required regular testing and blending in the plant to ensure that the blocks would properly solidify and not spoil.[89]

The strong connections the Cary Company had established in the Beauce Region of Quebec also extended across the U.S.-Canadian border into the adjacent maple forests of northern Somerset County, Maine. Although it was in the United States, this region of Maine was most accessible and closely connected with neighboring Quebec. When winter logging activities in these Maine woods came to an end each spring, farmers from Quebec would tap the maples of the area, producing hundreds of thousands of pounds of maple sugar. In the early 20th century this region was largely unsettled and rather wild, with no easy way to get the sugar to the American railroads for shipment. As a result, these Canadian sugarmakers brought the blocks of Beauce sugar back into Quebec to be stored in warehouses in St. George and Beauceville before clearing customs and being sold to the Cary Company and ultimately shipped by rail to St. Johnsbury.[90]

Cary's use of hundreds of buyers invariably led to encountering a wide range of individuals, some of which brought a certain flair or flavor to their endeavors. Clinton Cary told a story of one particular buyer from Quebec named Edward LaCroix. As Clinton Cary described it in a 1929 speech,

> He speaks very little broken English and runs a store in a village of not more than 10 houses. To go into the store, you would think that the building, stock and everything was not worth more than two or three thousand dollars, and yet through that store and some trading on the outside, like buying maple sugar, lambs, etc., he has accumulated at least half a million dollars.

The farmers come as far as 20 or 30 miles to trade with him when there are many stores much nearer.

In the spring when buying sugar, he uses his own capital and periodically sends us a bill for the sugar that he ships. He does not believe in paying the farmers by check but insists that it must be cash which he carries around in a little grip. I have driven with him 20 or 30 miles at midnight to get to the town where we loaded the next day and he has with him in the grip, as high as 30 or 40 thousand dollars in cash, which made me rather nervous.

Just this last spring, I left him at Black Lake in the middle of one afternoon. I was to meet him the next morning at Valley Junction, some 40 miles from there. He told me to get the money for the next day's work for him and to have it so he could use it the next morning and here is what he told me to do. The bank was closed so he had made arrangements to leave the money tied up in a newspaper, in a mall meat market. I went in and I told them that I wanted the package of maple sugar that had been left there for Ed. LaCroix. They went out in the back of the store in the refrigerator and brought out this package and gave it to me. The package contained $20,000.[91]

Setting prices for farmers in Quebec worked a little differently than in the United States in the early 20th century. Rather than the buyer agreeing to a price with each individual farmer, as was common with producers in the United States, in Quebec it was standard practice to meet with the farmers on Sunday on the steps of the church following the day's services. Proposed prices were presented by the buyers of whatever crop was in line for purchase, along with any necessary persuasive arguments that may assist the discussion. The farmers selling the products then conferred amongst themselves and decided collectively whether they would accept the price being offered or walk away. It was not uncommon, when faced with uncertainty or disagreement amongst the farmers to request the input of their priest, in which case, his "suggestion" was more-often-than-not the direction that they took.[92]

Packing Maple Sugar

If farmers are bothered about getting wooden packages to put their sugar in, they can put it in moulds made as follows: Cut a board 4 ft. x 8 in. for the bottom and two boards 4 ft. x 6 in. for sides; make eight grooves, one-quarter inch deep in each of the sides for partitions. These two side pieces can be fastened to the bottom board by three hinges. Make eight partitions to fit in the groves and the mould is complete. These moulds will make seven cakes weighing about ten pounds each and measuring 6 inches square.

This sugar must be cooked to 245 degrees and can be delivered to our agents in ordinary sugar or flour barrels. This will practically eliminate the cost of packages. We will pay the same price for this as for tub sugar and we will pay two cents a pound extra for sugar put up this way cooked to 265 degrees. This must be cooked hard enough so that it can be packed in burlap bags or bran sacks without dripping.

We can supply these moulds at $2.50 each made of spruce, or $2.00 made of hardwood. They will last for years.

CARY MAPLE SUGAR CO.
GEO. C. CARY, Mgr.

Figure 3.3: 1918 Packing Maple Sugar advert (Chronicling America website).

In April and May after the sugaring season was over, buying activities went into full swing. It was common for as much as 60 percent of the purchasing to be completed by the end of May and 90 percent of what would be bought to be done by the end of June. Buying agents were usually paid on commission around one half to one and half cents per pound of what they purchased.[93] As the sugaring season progressed and came to an end, producers and buyers shipped thousands of 55-gallon barrels to the St. Johnsbury factory with an average of 10 to 12 rail cars arriving at the plant each day. On especially busy days, as many as 40 cars arrived at the plant for storage and processing.[94]

In an effort to maintain quality control along with a desire to receive an orderly, uniform product from their sugarmakers, the Cary Company sometimes gave advice and rather explicit directions in ads placed in local newspapers stating how to prepare the sugar, build sugar molds, and pack sugar for sale and shipment. It is notable to see from the ad in Figure 3.3 which demonstrates how the company was willing to pay a premium of two cents a pound more for higher quality tub sugar that was cooked to a temperature of 265 degrees and had more moisture removed than for moist sugar packed in burlap sacks dripping with syrup.[95]

Partnering with Maple Royalty – Towle's Log Cabin Syrup

The Towle Maple Products Company of St. Paul, Minnesota, best known as the makers of Towle's Log Cabin Syrup, opened a bottling operation for their blended cane and maple syrups in Cary's Bay Street facility in St. Johnsbury in April of 1910. Their appearance in St. Johnsbury was a direct result of George Cary selling the maple syrup portion of his business to the Towle Company, while retaining the maple sugar component (Figure 3.4). With the sale to Towle's, beginning in 1910, Cary stopped purchasing bulk syrup to reform into blocks and only purchased maple sugar for processing and resale. The Towle Company purchase of the Cary facility in St. Johnsbury is not entirely a surprise, when one realizes that George Cary was a member of their board of directors. At this time, Towle's St. Johnsbury connection to the Cary Company was solidified with the announcement that John Rickaby, then the Vice President of the Cary Company, would be moving to a key management position in Towle's new operation.[96]

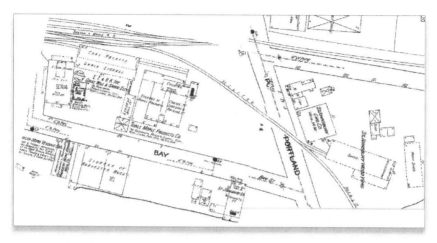

Figure 3.4: 1912 Sanborn fire insurance map composite showing Towle's location and St. Johnsbury Grocery, Cary's new location (Courtesy of Library of Congress).

Selling the maple syrup portion of their operation and Bay Street facility to the Towle Company left the Cary Maple Sugar Company without a home and without much of the equipment they had used in packing maple syrup since their existing set-up was sold in its entirety to the Towle Company. The Cary Company responded by immediately purchasing the nearby St. Johnsbury Grocery (See Figure 2.12). With this purchase of the grocery building, the Cary Company only had to relocate a few hundred yards to the north at the west end of Portland Street (Figures 3.5 and 3.6). Selling the maple syrup portion of the company to Towle meant that the Cary Company, for the time being, was focused exclusively on the buying, reprocessing, and selling of maple sugar.[97]

The Towle Company wasted no time in getting its new operation up and running, rapidly expanding the scale of the facilities they purchased from Cary. In fact, during a St. Johnsbury visit from Towle Company President P.J. Towle in March of 1910, it was announced that with the purchase they would also be remodeling and expanding the Bay Street plant, installing a new boiler and adding eight new boiling kettles. The following year, the Towle Company was operating at full capacity from seven in the morning to midnight most evenings.

Figure 3.5: Postcard image showing Towle's name on old Cary Maple building and new Cary building to the right (Author's Collection).

Figure 3.6: Close up of Postcard showing Cary Company Building and Towle's Building.

Their modernized packing plant was a bustling operation as outlined in a 1911 St. Johnsbury Caledonian article:

> The maple syrup which has been purchased from the farmer is placed in two 250 gallon and four 150-gallon copper kettles. This sugar is remelted by steam until it

has reached the correct specific gravity and then it is pumped through a filter press which removes any dirt or nitre which may be in the sugar, into four large storage tanks which have a capacity of 550 gallons each. Then, as needed, it is piped downstairs to copper kettles where it is reheated by steam and then passes into the filling machine which fills six receptacles of any kind at the same time. From there the syrup passes to the capping machine which automatically caps the can or bottle with the crown stopper or to another machine which corks the receptacles as the case may be.[98]

The Towle Company continued to expand their St. Johnsbury operation. In April of 1913 the Towle Company moved out of Cary's former location on Bay Street into an adjacent 50 by 150-foot, two-story brick fireproof building, known as the Pillsbury Baldwin Plant.

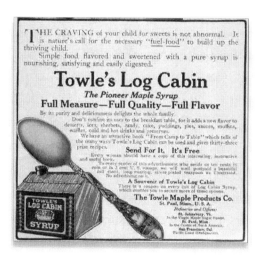

Figure 3.7: Log Cabin advertisement (Author's Collection).

The building was constructed only two years earlier along the same railroad lines as Cary and Towle's first Bay Street building by the Pillsbury-Baldwin Company, a manufacturer of bathroom fixtures. This larger new location allowed the Towle Company to load as many as twelve rail cars a day.⁹⁹ During this period of the Towle Company's residence in St. Johnsbury, nearly all their national advertisements, syrup cans, and syrup bottles noted that St. Johnsbury, along with St. Paul and San Francisco, were the home locations of the company (Figure 3.7). Such an announcement, along with Cary's growing maple sugar empire, went a long way towards further solidifying St. Johnsbury as the Maple Center of the World. In addition to the famous and still active Log Cabin syrup label, the Towle Company also sported a Vermont Maid label and a Crown of Canada label on metal cans and glass bottles. The Towle's Vermont Maid label was different from the other Vermont Maid brand of syrup bottled out of Burlington by the Penick and Ford company. Such bottles from the Towle's era in St. Johnsbury are highly valued by collectors.

By 1912 the Cary Company had grown to a size where it was conducting a million dollars in transactions a year in buying and selling only maple sugar. At the same time, the Towle Maple Products Company was also doing a million dollars'-worth of maple syrup business out of St. Johnsbury, and together at that time, these businesses arguably made St. Johnsbury the largest maple sugar and syrup market in the world.¹⁰⁰

However, St. Johnsbury's role as a home to Log Cabin Syrup was short lived. A few years later, following the death of their president and founder P. J. Towle in 1915, the Towle Maple Products Company went through a change in management, and announced that they would close their St. Johnsbury bottling plant and move their operation to Chicago.¹⁰¹ Towle's leaving St. Johnsbury re-opened the market for Cary to get back into the business of buying maple syrup as well as maple sugar, an opportunity he soon put to good use with a new emphasis on buying maple syrup in barrels as discussed earlier.

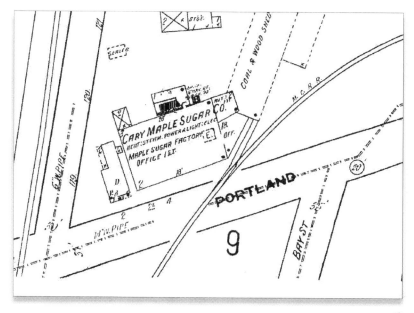

Figure 3.8: 1919 Sanborn fire insurance map close-up showing Cary at St. Johnsbury Grocery location (Courtesy of Library of Congress).

Figure 3.9: Photo of St. Johnsbury Grocery next to Cary letterhead showing grocery building during Cary occupation (Author's Collection).

Following the departure of Towle's, the Cary Company continued to occupy the St. Johnsbury Grocery building and even expanded it in 1917, adding a 28 foot by 50-foot, two-story addition to the west side, with this expanded building later being locally referred to as the Cary Block (Figure 3.8).[102] Along with the expansion of the building, a concrete foundation was laid in the basement of the existing building. Conveniently located adjacent to the tracks, Cary installed company offices upstairs and sugar and syrup handling facilities below on the first floor. Cary even featured the building on its company letterhead at the time (Figure 3.9). The Cary Company continued to occupy this building as office space until 1929 when they moved all offices into their new two-story brick Maple Grove Candies building on the east end of Portland Street in front of the four-story Cary factory discussed later in this chapter. Today the former Cary Company/St. Johnsbury Grocery building is still standing but is largely hidden from view under the Portland Street overpass, which was constructed in 1943.

Arrival of Maple Grove Candies
The departure of Towle's Log Cabin Syrup from St. Johnsbury in 1915 did not threaten the town's claim to the title of Maple Capital of the World, since the very same year marked the arrival of Maple Grove Candies and a new chapter in the town's ongoing maple story.

Figure 3.10: Home of Katherine Ide Gray known as "Waysides" (Courtesy of St. Johnsbury History and Heritage Center).

Maple Grove Candies began in July of that year as a summer endeavor of high school student Helen Gray and her friend Ethel McLaren. Working in the kitchen of the Gray family farm located three miles south of St. Johnsbury on the road to the village of Passumpsic, these women experimented with different recipes of their own design for the perfect maple candies.[103] After a few months of trial and error, word spread that they were in the candy business and orders began coming in. These orders came first as a trickle, but soon after came as a regular stream. Helen Gray's mother, Katherine Ide Gray, had been extremely supportive of their work from the beginning and saw to it that they had room to work, converting a shed into a candy kitchen at the Gray farm, then known as "The Wayside." Interest in their candies grew and additional work space was provided (see Figure 2.13 and Figure 3.10).[104] At some point in their first year the three women settled on the name Maple Grove Candies.

Figure 3.11: 1915 Maple Grove Candies Advertisement in St. Johnsbury Caledonian (Chronicling America website).

As a full-fledged candy business was born, the elder of the trio, Katherine Ide Gray, became fully involved in guiding the growing enterprise. Ultimately, Katherine's daughter Helen Gray graduated from high school, married, and went on to Columbia University where she studied home economics, and Ethel McLaren became a nurse, but not before both young entrepreneurs got a taste of business success.[105]

The new candy business advertised the use of attractive ingredients like fresh cream and butternuts as well as maple sugar in their candies and encouraged people to request a box of samples right away. Maple Grove Candies even placed an advertisement on the front page of the St. Johnsbury *Caledonian* requesting children gather butternuts and sell then to Maple Grove Candies for use in making their candies (Figure 3.11).[106]

Figure 3.12: Helen Gray making candies (Courtesy of the St. Johnsbury History and Heritage Center).

One of the secrets to Maple Grove Candies success was a technique they developed for preserving and texturing their molded maple cream candies. Each candy was dipped in a solution of maple syrup that contained suspended sugar particles. This solution with particles created a kind of textured coating on the exterior of the candies that kept the candy from drying out quickly, keeping the maple cream interior soft for longer periods of time (Figure 3.12).[107]

The success of Maple Grove Candies was quick and welcomed, and by January, 1920 the small home-based operation became a full-fledged corporation: Maple Grove Candies, Incorporated. As might be expected, the principal founders of Maple Grove Candies, Katherine Ide Gray, Helen Gray Powell, and Ethel McLaren, stepped into leadership roles for the new corporation, with Katherine Ide Gray serving as the President and general manager. However, a new addition to their ranks and their newly formed board of directors was the involvement of George C. Cary, due to his significant role in the company's capitalization and his influence and assistance in national sales and marketing of maple products. Maple Grove Candies, Incorporated was launched with $100,000 of capitalization, provided by an agglomeration of investors including the original founders of the Gray's and Mrs. McLaren, George Cary but also with the assistance of George Cary's personal secretary Gertrude M. Franklin, and three women from the Mary Elizabeth Candies Company of New York, namely Mary Elizabeth Evans, Fanny Reigal Evans, and Fanny Reigal Evans, Jr. Mary Elizabeth Evans was selected as the Vice President and Charles W. Ruiter was chosen to be the clerk and treasurer.[108]

Although the Mary Elizabeth Candies company was well established throughout New England and North America, its involvement with Maple Grove Candies was purely as a shareholder. Mary Elizabeth Candies was not looking to expand into the maple candy business. In the years prior to and following the incorporation of Maple Grove Candies, Mary Elizabeth Evans herself visited the St. Johnsbury area during the sugaring season and toured the Cary Company facilities, observing the sugaring process, and enjoyed time as a guest at George Cary's North Danville farm. Evans was also described as a "frequent visitor" to the original Maple Grove Candies facility at the Gray's "Wayside" farm.[109]

It was initially planned that the newly incorporated Maple Grove Candies would move into the Cary Company's location in the old St. Johnsbury Grocery building, upon the completion and move of the Cary Company into their new factory, then under construction on Portland Street in St. Johnsbury. However, for reasons unknown, this plan changed and a few months later it was announced that Maple Grove Candies would be moving to the Pinehurst Mansion near downtown St. Johnsbury. Pinehurst was the unoccupied mansion and estate built in 1852 for Horace Fairbanks, the former Governor of Vermont and son of Erastus Fairbanks, the founder of the Fairbanks scales empire (Figure 3.13).[110]

Figure 3.13: Maple Grove Inn at Pinehurst Mansion in real photo post card (Author's Collection).

The move of Maple Grove Candies out of the Gray farm and into the Fairbanks' Pinehurst Mansion was facilitated by George Cary who personally purchased the property for Maple Grove Candies in June of 1920. Cary purchased the fifteen-acre property from the Gillman brothers who earlier purchased it from Theodora Willard, the granddaughter and heir of Horace Fairbanks. The prominent Fairbanks home and gardens sat atop a hill on St. Johnsbury's Western Avenue and had languished unused for several years. Cary was interested in seeing it preserved intact. In covering the $11,500 price tag, Cary paid $4900 in cash and mortgaged the remainder.

Figure 3.14: Interior kitchen at Pinehurst Mansion (Courtesy of the St Johnsbury History and Heritage Center).

Cary further divided the grounds of the estate, with the mansion going to Maple Grove Candies, the deer park was sold to Gertrude Franklin and the title to the remainder of the grounds stayed in Cary's hands. However, the purchase was not without conditions aimed at protecting the open space and beauty of the grounds around the mansion. In particular, the deed stated that no buildings were to be built on the lots adjacent to the Athenaeum or the flower garden or adjacent to Western Avenue or Main Street. If for some reason Cary felt he needed to sell his remaining portion of the property, Maple Grove Candies had the first right to buy.[111]

Figure 3.15: Two women making candy at Maple Grove Inn (Courtesy of the Fairbanks Museum and Planetarium).

The opening day of the new Maple Grove Candies operation at the Pinehurst Mansion on Thursday, December 9th, 1920 witnessed over 1,000 visitors. An advertisement on the front page of the St. Johnsbury *Caledonian Record* invited visitors to attend and tour the new facilities.[112] With the opening of business at Pinehurst, Maple Grove Candies not only expanded its production facilities but also entered a new phase of business with their Maple Grove Tea Room. The tea room was targeted at tourists looking to stop along their travels along the new Theodore Roosevelt Highway, now known as US Highway 2, and as a meeting place for local social functions for the people of St. Johnsbury. The front parlor rooms of the house were reserved for the tea room and social space. The popularity of the tea room further led to the addition of the Maple Grove Inn a few years later, with overnight accommodations and guest rooms in the mansion for travelers wishing to stop for the night.

In the back of the house and upper floors, the candy manufacturing rooms were painted all white and the young women employed in the candy making aspects of the company dressed in white caps and buff colored uniforms (Figures 3.14 and 3.15). The special ingredients, such as barrels of maple sugar, nuts, and cane sugar were stored in the basement, whereas the maple syrup was heated in kettles on the first floor. Numerous gas stoves, ovens, stirring and dipping machines, and other necessary equipment were found on the first and second floor kitchens where the many confections were made and handled. As a modernized and efficient work place in 1920, all the rooms were connected by speaking tubes and all the rooms were heated and well lit.[113]

Maple Grove Candies' ongoing popularity and success, along with their move to the new Pinehurst location and the expansion of their operations, was demonstrated by their having over 10,000 visitors to their Pinehurst facility in 1922 alone. During their busy holiday season as many as 30 women were employed preparing, packaging, and shipping many tons of candy around the United States and overseas.[114]

Riding the wave of the success of their Maple Grove Tea Room in St. Johnsbury, the Grays expanded the hospitality area of their business. Under the separate corporate name of Maple Grove Products, Inc., The Grays opened the Maple Grove Restaurant in New York City around 1925 (Figure 3.16). Helen Gray, now Helen Gray Powell, and her husband Harold Gates Powell moved to New York City to manage the restaurant. Located at 206 West 57th Street, the Maple Grove Restaurant featured pancakes and Vermont maple syrup and enticed customers to experience "A Little New England in New York."[115] A menu for the restaurant painted the picture with these words - "The hills of Vermont are famed for their maple sugar. And so, at the Maple Grove Restaurant you may enjoy dishes with the true flavor of maple syrup as well as many other appetizing foods. From the furnishings and mural decorations, one gets the atmosphere and feeling of the great Vermont woods, truly a breath of old Vermont in New York."[116]

Lunch at the New York restaurant was available for between seventy-five cents and one dollar and dinner was available for as low as one dollar and as high as two dollars. The interior of the restaurant was painted with a series of murals featuring activities in the sugarbush, including a sugar house, pails on trees and the gathering of sap with a horse-drawn sled (Figure 3.16).

Figure 3.16: Interior of Maple Grove Tea Room in New York City (Courtesy of the Fairbanks Museum and Planetarium).

Over the years the company made and sold boxes of maple candies, maple chocolates, bon-bons, granulated maple sugar, maple cream, pure maple syrup in glass and tin, and fancy and novelty gift sets like faux wooden books, a miniature firkin or pail, and a log cabin. Some of the most popular items were the small maple sugar candies in the shapes of maple leaves and fruits, and the larger candies in the shapes of a soldier, a maiden, a maple man, and Santa Claus.[117]

Erecting a Fortress - The St. Johnsbury Plant

The act of Maple Grove Candies taking up residence in the Pinehurst Mansion was big news in St. Johnsbury in 1920. What was even bigger news the year before was the construction of a large modern factory on the edge of town for the ever-growing Cary Maple Sugar Company. Cary took full advantage of his business and social connections in St.

Johnsbury when laying out plans in the summer of 1919 to build a new modern plant for his company. Cary enlisted the support of the influential St. Johnsbury Commercial Club, which Cary rather conveniently was not only a member, but also a recent club president. Cary's proposal included a request for a ten-year tax break for the plant should he agree to build in St. Johnsbury, promising work for as many as one hundred men. In a speech to the Commercial Club, Cary shared that other towns had made him offers with enticements, but he started the company in St. Johnsbury and, considering St. Johnsbury his home, would like to keep it in St. Johnsbury.[118]

The commercial club came out in force in support of not only the building proposal, but more importantly, the proposed tax break, with one member stating, "even if George Cary was previously unknown to him and a complete stranger, he would support the proposal that was put in front of him." Commercial Club support was unanimous and included a petition presented to the town selectmen requesting a town meeting to hear and discuss the tax break proposal. The Commercial Club's position was splashed across the front page of the *Evening Caledonian* with the top headline reading "CARY OFFERS NEW FACTORY TO EMPLOY 100 MEN."[119]

It was Cary's intention that with a new and expanded operation in St. Johnsbury they would triple their capacity and most of their syrup and sugar would be processed at the new factory. Such growth would mean filling three to four rail cars with block sugar per day for an annual shipment of hundreds of rail cars.[120]

A town meeting was scheduled for the taxpayers of St. Johnsbury to vote on the tax-exemption proposal and in the week before the editors of the *Evening Caledonian* came out with a "press comment," and a plea to "make it unanimous", in support of the proposal. On the afternoon of Saturday, September 22, 1919 over 100 voters attended the special Town Hall meeting and voted unanimously in support of a ten-year tax break in exchange for construction of a new Cary Maple Sugar Company plant in St. Johnsbury.[121]

In the fall of 1919, preparation of the site for construction began at the east end of the village on land sandwiched between Portland Avenue and a bend in the Moose River. Two new parallel railroad spurs off the Maine Central Railroad were installed for the exclusive use by the plant on which 15 to 20 rail cars could be parked at a time. A wood framed storehouse for storing empty barrels with a dimension of 110 by 40 feet was built alongside the railroad spurs west of the plant.[122] A box shop was located to the west of the storehouse and was described as a long wooden building painted barn-red.[123]

Figure 3.17: Cary plant postcard ca. 1920 (Author's Collection).

The main plant was four-stories tall and 60 by 200 feet in dimension, with the addition of a one-story wing that was 39 by 36 feet in dimension. Rising high above the buildings was a brick chimney over 100 feet tall (Figure 3.17). The plant was designed by engineering firm Webster & Libby of Portland, Maine and constructed under the direction of general contractor H.P. Cummings Construction Company of Woodsville, New Hampshire with the heating and plumbing work awarded to C.H. Goss & Company of St. Johnsbury. The roofing and metal work went to

Henry H. Salls of Burlington, Vermont.[124] The original contracts for construction amounted to $100,000.[125] The building boasted a fireproof design of reinforced concrete framing interlaced with brick facing (Figure 3.18).[126] A significant feature of the plant were the four large 1,200-gallon steam heated copper tanks for boiling maple syrup to proper temperatures and consistencies prior to packing as solid maple sugar. Wooden boxes from the box shop were transported to the plant via conveyor belt.

After being prepared in the kettles on an upper floor, semi-liquid maple sugar was poured into wax paper lined wooden boxes, whereby it would harden in the boxes to form "Highland Block" sugar for shipment to tobacco firms and blenders.[127] Construction of the plant continued through 1920 and the plant began operation in March of 1921.[128] Expansion of the plant continued over the years as additional warehouses were added, including a 116 by 40-foot extension of their initial warehouse.[129]

Figure 3.18: Interior of Cary warehouse (Courtesy of Tom Olson and New England Maple Museum).

The workforce at the Cary plant through the 1920s was nearly all male with the men handling the processing and packaging equipment, neatly dressed in clean white cotton uniforms. The sterile, near medical appearance of this industrialized operation was in great contrast to the often gritty and rustic interiors of many of the sugarhouses from which the maple syrup and sugar they were reprocessing had originated.

In the early 1920s the Cary Company plant often operated at full-steam for only part of the year. The tall brick chimney on the southeast side of the plant bellowed thick black smoke when the boilers were in operation. By the late 1920s and with the expansion of the company's product lines beyond "Highland Block" to include pure maple syrup in cans and bottles of various sizes, the plant was a bustling place and in operation all twelve months of the year. However, processing blocks of sugar for flavoring and blending continued to form the bulk of the company's business. To emphasize the continued importance of block sugaring for flavoring tobacco, Clinton Cary, then an assistant manager at the company, stated in a speech to the St. Johnsbury Rotary Club that one (unnamed) tobacco company alone was buying over 5 million pounds of maple sugar a year to flavor one single brand of cigarettes.[130]

The Cary Company also owned and operated a sawmill in the woods behind their plant. This mill was accessed by a small bridge and across the Moose River and was primarily tasked with supplying the lumber for the box shop. This shop produced the nearly endless supply of wooden boxes needed by the Cary Company to pack the 30 and 70-pound blocks of sugar for shipment to the tobacco companies and syrup blenders.

The new Cary facilities established at the eastern end of St. Johnsbury were not limited to the four-story factory, warehouses and sawmill along the railroad tracks. Like the women at Maple Grove Candies, Cary was also interested in the hospitality business and recognized the value of the location for capturing the attention and patronage of passing motorists entering St. Johnsbury along the adjacent U.S. Highway 2. To promote his company and products and add another dimension to the company portfolio Cary established the Maple Inn Tea Room and the Maple Cabin Inn enterprises.

Maple Inn Tea Room

As a venture of the Cary Maple Sugar Company, this log cabin styled building was installed directly in front of the Cary Company plant. Work on the cabin was quickly completed and the Maple Inn Tea Room (not to be confused with the Maple Grove Tea Room) opened in August of 1920, months before the adjacent plant was completed and began operation.[131] In Figure 3.19, one can see the plant under construction in the background behind the finished Maple Inn Tea Room. In these early years the Maple Inn Tea Room was opened as a tea room, wayside restaurant, and gift shop along Portland Street in St. Johnsbury. In later years, the food service was replaced with an expanded gift shop.

Figure 3.19: Maple Inn Tea Room with Cary plant under construction in background (Author's Collection).

The Maple Inn Tea Room described itself in a brochure as a "cozy Tea Room, famous for its good food at fair prices." Built with a full kitchen in the basement and access to the first-floor dining room by a dumb waiter style lift, one could enjoy waffles with pure maple syrup, the "best coffee you ever tasted," along with maple ice cream and other menu items.

Figure 3.20: Postcard of Maple Cabin interior first view (Author's Collection).

Figure 3.21: Postcard of Maple Cabin interior second view (Author's Collection).

Of course, maple sugar and maple syrup were available for sale, along with Maple Grove Candies and other unique gifts such as "authentic," Navajo rugs and balsam pillows (Figures 3.20 and Figure 3.21).[132] Over the years thousands of postcards of the Maple Inn Tea Room have been mailed home from St. Johnsbury by tourists that stopped in each year.

Maple Cabin Inn

The Maple Cabin Inn was another venture by Cary designed to promote the company and capture the business of travelers coming to and through St. Johnsbury. Located directly across U.S. Highway 2 from the Maple Inn Tea Room and the new Cary Company plant, the Maple Cabin Inn advertised itself as "just the right place to stay overnight."

Figure 3.22: Postcard of Maple Cabin Inn from road (Author's Collection).

It boasted an attractive log cabin, and old-fashioned flower garden, a lobby with a fire place, and rooms with baths and Simmons beds and Beauty Rest mattresses (Figure 3.22).[133] Josephine Cary Smith, the cousin of George Cary, came to St. Johnsbury following the death of her husband and was the proprietor of the Maple Cabin Inn from 1928 until at least 1939. It is unclear how long the Maple Cabin Inn continued to operate for paying guests. The Cary company continued to own the property through multiple changes in its corporate ownership and in later years used it for accommodations for company business and as a residential rental property.

Establishment of a Northern Outpost - Lennoxville Plant

Expansion of the company's footprint was not limited to St. Johnsbury. Notable new construction also occurred in Quebec. For a few years in the 1920s, the Cary Company operated a small warehouse about 90 miles (140 km) to north in Sherbrooke, Quebec (see Figure 2.1). Business was booming in Quebec and the Cary Company was pushing its Quebec producers to shift to selling their syrup in barrels and move away from producing and selling blocks and chucks of Beauce sugar. With a growing volume of syrup in drums, the company was ready to locate and operate a sister factory in Quebec rather than ship the barrels to St. Johnsbury for processing.

In 1929 the Cary Company expanded its presence in Quebec with the construction of a new, three-story plant on College Street in Lennoxville, a suburb of Sherbrooke, Quebec. Situated adjacent to the Canadian Pacific Railway and the Canadian National Railway, this new reinforced concrete plant was virtually identical in appearance to Cary's St. Johnsbury plant built in 1920 (Figure 3.23). Robert M. Boright was hired as the plant manager.[134]

The Cary Company purchased the twenty-five-acre Lennoxville site for $10,000 from the Canadian Pacific Railroad. The Lennoxville plant featured a 100 by 8-foot three-story, reinforced concrete and brick trimmed building, along with a 260 by 80-foot steel-sided warehouse adjacent to the south elevation. Like the St. Johnsbury plant it was modelled upon, the Lennoxville plant boasted a fire-prevention sprinkler system, two freight elevators, two large boilers fired by crude oil, and a 125-foot tall brick chimney (Figure 3.24).[135]

Figure 3.23: Photo of Cary plant in Lennoxville, Quebec (Courtesy of LAHMS Archives).

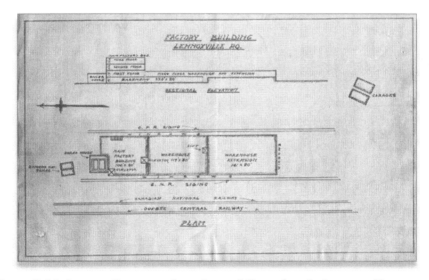

Figure 3.24: Image of construction plans of Cary plant in Lennoxville, Quebec (Courtesy of LAHMS Archives).

Inside the plant the company installed state of the art equipment for the rapid and sanitary storage, handling, cooking, and packing of massive volumes of maple syrup. Two 10,000-gallon and two 5,000-gallon steel tanks were used to store syrup, and three 1,500-gallon steam jacketed tanks for heating syrup. There were also large volume filter presses, and washing, sterilizing, bottling, and canning equipment.[136] With the construction of the Lennoxville plant, it was intended that all export business to British markets and British clients would be handed in Quebec. This is because the commerce would be between British Possessions, and the company could then avoid paying U.S. to Britain duties on such transactions.[137]

Despite the effort and expense of opening the plant in Lennoxville, the Cary years of operation at the plant were short-lived and the plant was sold two years later as part of the bankruptcy reorganization in 1931. Robert Boright, former plant manager, established his own company, Quebec Maple Products, LTD, and purchased the plant. Quebec Maple Products did not occupy the building for very long either and moved to another location in 1933 before selling the plant to the Quebec Asbestos Corporation in 1934. In 1935 the Phillip Carey Manufacturing Company out of Cincinnati purchased the plant for the manufacture of asbestos coverings until a fire destroyed the plant in December 1967.[138]

As new maple sugaring ventures sprung up around Vermont and especially St. Johnsbury, Cary often found a way to have a hand in their operation and expansion. In fifteen short years, the Cary Company was buying and selling more maple sugar and syrup than any other company in North America and controlled an estimated four-fifths of bulk sugar and syrup made in the United States. His knowledge and influence in the industry was sought out as was his financial support. Such involvement allowed Cary to always know what the competition was doing. If a venture failed, he would be there to pick up the pieces, as with Towle's Maple Products Company, if it succeeded he was there to share in their spoils as with Maple Grove Candies. Although Cary didn't know it at the time, the success of Maple Grove Candies would become important to the future survival of the Cary Company in the coming decades.

Even with an ongoing expansion into Quebec, Cary maintained a focus on his American operations, concentrating his base of operations in St. Johnsbury. Cary presented a physical manifestation of his power and influence with the construction of his four-story factory and related Maple Inn Tea Room and a Maple Cabin Inn guest house in St. Johnsbury followed with the near mirror-image sister factory in Lennoxville, Quebec. With his business literally and figuratively on solid grounds and no one stepping up to challenge him, his empire was secure. Cary was poised to spread his maple related interests even wider while promoting the industry and the products of Vermont.

4

Growing the King's Army

Control of the bulk market in the maple sugar industry was firmly in the hands of the Cary Company by the early 1920s. With that, Cary spent the next decade diversifying production and expanding his reach. George Cary and the company began to actively promote the sales of their products and label for home consumption, such as with the introduction of Highland Brand Pure Maple Syrup. In other arenas, Cary was a significant backer and participant in a multi-year state promotional railroad tour known as the *Vermont Maple Sugar Special* and went so far as to have a promotional silent movie staged and filmed in his Highland Farm sugarbush and St. Johnsbury plant. Likewise, the Cary Company further diversified its holdings and product beyond the sales of bulk sugar, purchasing the Maple Grove Candies, forming the Vermont Maple Sugar Company, promoting the Brower Pipeline System, and absorbing the failed Vermont Maple Syrup Producers Cooperative Exchange.

Brower Pipeline System
Being a wise businessman, George Cary was not afraid to experiment with new and innovative technology, and more efficient methods of making, moving, and processing maple sugar. In this regard, it was no surprise that, following a short trial season in 1918, Cary embraced and

fully promoted the use and manufacture of a new metal pipeline system that would replace the traditional pails and tanks for gathering maple sap, going so far as to partner with the inventor and open a manufacturing operation in St. Johnsbury (Figure 4.1).[139] The Brower Sap Piping System, as it was formally known, was invented by sugarmaker, tinsmith, and inventor William C. Brower near Gloversville, New York. The pipeline system was a series of interlocking galvanized tin tubes that were suspended from heavy wire strung throughout a sugarbush to carry fresh maple sap down slope directly from a tap in the maple tree to a collection tank at the base of the slope or at the sugarhouse (Figure 4.2).

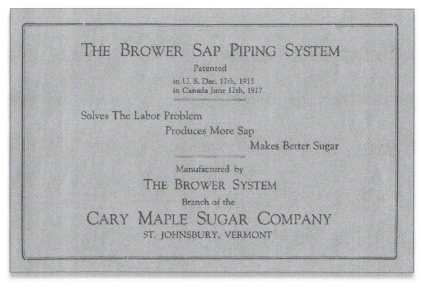

Figure 4.1: Brower pipeline sales booklet (Courtesy of Hale Mattoon).

The system often went by the nickname of the "gooseneck system" in reflection of the system's metal spout and attached downspout that resembled the shape of a goose's body and long neck. Patented in 1916, the system was a precursor to the modern plastic tubing seen throughout sugarbushes today (Figure 4.2). While slightly more labor intensive to install than the pails most common at that time, the pipeline system effectively eliminated the time consuming and costly need to gather sap by foot from each tree, as well as the use of teams of oxen or horses pulling gathering tanks on sleds or wagons.[140]

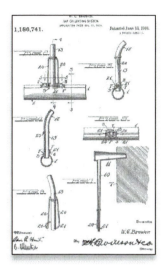

Figure 4.2: United States Patent No. 1,186,741 awarded to Jacob Brower (United States Patent Office website).

In the sugarbushes at both his Pine Lodge Farm, and at his Highland Farm Cary installed thousands of feet of the Brower system to gather sap from over 16000 trees.[141] Convinced of its effectiveness and value, in 1920 the Cary Company went into partnership with Brower, bringing him from his upstate New York home to St. Johnsbury to lead production of the metal tubing on a greater scale. Working with a crew of ten men in a small shop in St. Johnsbury and financed by the Cary Company, enough Goosenecks were fabricated to tap over 50,000 trees in the 1920 season. Orders for the 1921 season were slated to produce tubing to tap over 200,000 trees.[142] The Cary Company published a booklet in 1920 explaining the use of the system along with testimonials from Vermont sugarmakers that had made the shift to the system.[143] Cary featured the installation and use of the piping system in the 1927 film made in his Highland Farm sugarbush (Figure 4.3).

Spreading the word of the availability and success of this invention, Cary and Brower promoted the system at the 1920 Caledonian County Fair. The Cary Company's exhibit on the midway featured a display and demonstration of the Brower Sap Piping System.

Figure 4.3: Brower pipeline in use in Cary Sugarbush (Author's Collection).

As a new branch of the Cary Company, they were eager to share and promote this new technology. On hand to demonstrate the system was Roy E. Davis, the manager of the Company's pipeline business. The display demonstrating the system "consisted of a miniature sugar house, surrounded by maple trees and the Brower pipes attached to each tree and all connecting with the main pipe that runs into the sugar house".[144]

The system was adopted primarily in Vermont, New York and New Hampshire, but also made it into use as far west as Wisconsin.[145] How, why, and when production of the tubing system ceased in St. Johnsbury is not entirely clear. It appears that the manufacturing operation in St. Johnsbury continued into the mid-1920s, after which William C. Brower returned to his home and sugarbush in New York. In fact, Brower's New

York neighbors and their descendants, who had been among the very first to test and use the system for sap gathering continue to install a small amount of the Brower System each spring.[146]

Movie Making

Wishing to display both the evolution of sap gathering and maple sugar making as well as the modern process employed by the Cary Maple Sugar Company, George Cary arranged for a silent moving picture to be made in 1927. The film included outdoor scenes from the sugarbush and sugarhouses at Cary's Highland Farm, along with action shots of processing and packing syrup and sugar in the Cary Company plant in St. Johnsbury. Today, a copy of the film, which was originally shot on 35 mm nitrate stock, has been archived in the Philippe Beaudry Collection at Northeast Historic Film, a repository in Bucksport, Maine.[147]

The silent moving picture, along with an extensive collection of still photographs of the same sugarbush and sugarhouse scenes as featured in the film, were shot over several days by well-known photographers Harry and Alice Richardson of Newport, Vermont. The Richardson's were widely regarded for their many outdoor and studio photographs of the Northeast Kingdom in Vermont, including a variety of colorful novelty postcards. It was announced as early as 1926 that the Richardson's would be making a moving picture for the Cary Maple Sugar Company.[148]

Scenes in the sugarbush focused on three romanticized periods in the history of maple sugaring; Native American sugaring, nineteenth century Euro-American/Euro-Canadian sugaring, and early twentieth century Euro-American/Euro-Canadian sugaring. For the telling of the Native American story, Cary hired a full-blooded Penobscot Indian named John Lewey from Old Town, Maine (Figure 4.4). Mr. Lewey was accompanied by his son Roy Lewey.
Posing in the snow in a full-feathered Plains Indian-style headdress, buckskins, and polished leather dress shoes, Lewey is shown tapping a few maple trees, gathering sap with wood pails from wood troughs, and

boiling sap in a large iron kettle suspended from a tripod in front of a newly constructed log cabin. Sap was gathered from about one hundred split log wood troughs fed by hand carved flat wood taps.[149]

Figure 4.4: John Lewey as Penobscot Indian in Cary silent film (Courtesy of Tom Olson and New England Maple Museum).

The nineteenth century methods of sugaring featured a Yankee farmer played by Albert Leland, himself a sugarmaker from Barton, Vermont (Figure 4.5). Leland was dressed for the part, complete with wide brimmed straw hat, a thick full-length beard, and high boots. Equipped with a shoulder yoke and two wooden gathering pails, Leland was shown hustling from tree to tree collecting sap from wood collecting pails set on the ground and transporting it to a gathering tank pulled by oxen through the snow.[150] A young Richard Franklin, son of Earl Franklin, a Cary employee, was shown leading a pair of steers with a goad stick (Figure 4.6), while in another scene, Mr. Cary himself appears driving a different pair of oxen along a road in the sugarbush (Figure 4.8).

Figure 4.5: Albert Leland as New England Yankee in Cary silent film (Courtesy of Tom Olson and New England Maple Museum).

Twentieth century sugaring was depicted both with the collection of sap in covered galvanized metal pails hung from the trees along with the cutting-edge Brower Sap Piping System. In one scene a man is shown installing the Gooseneck section of the Brower pipeline in a taphole in the tree. Later he is shown connecting sections of the pipeline along their wire supports, while in another he is walking along and checking the metal pipeline for leaks.

There are also numerous scenes of Cary's Highland Farm sugarhouses in action with steam billowing from the cupola, men feeding the boiling arches and drawing off syrup. Other men are seen moving barrels of syrup, along with gathering and unloading tanks of fresh sap pulled on sleds by teams of Cary's prized oxen.

Besides the footage of the sap gathering and syrup making process in the sugarbush and sugarhouses, the filmmakers also shot footage inside Cary's St. Johnsbury plant. Such shots included a worker filling wooden boxes lined with waxed paper on a conveyor line with thick hot maple sugar from an overhead vat as well as a room full of hundreds of such boxes of sugar in a warehouse cooling.

Figure 4.6: Young Richard Franklin leading team of oxen in Cary silent film (Courtesy of Tom Olson and New England Maple Museum).

In contrast to the dirt and soot of the scenes from the sugarbush and sugarhouses, the shots from the plant interior feature employees clad in all white smocks and hats working with processing and automated packing equipment in a sterile-like white painted and polished interior. Shipping boxes labelled "Highland Pure Maple" are shown being nailed together and one scene a worker displays a can of "Highland Pure Maple Syrup".

One-part marketing tool and one-part educational materials, the film was likely shown in theaters as a short before feature films began. A few years after the shooting of the film, a reporter from the Caledonian Record who had been on hand to document the movie making told of his delight at seeing the film while in a movie house in Seattle, Washington. The reporter was even more shocked to see a few seconds

of himself on the film where they had captured
drinking fresh sap from a metal collection pail b

Maple Sugar Train
Begun in May 1926 as the idea of Harry C. W
VT, the "Vermont Maple Sugar Special" was a
showcasing Vermont and its products and re   , with special
attention to it maple sugar production[152]. George Cary was a keen
supporter of the train, proudly representing his company, St. Johnsbury,
and the State of Vermont. Initially operating on an eleven-day tour of 21
cities in the northeast, the train featured nine Pullman cars and four
exhibition cars, as well as three baggage cars, one of which was filled with
maple sugar packages from the Cary Company to be given away as gifts
and sold along the way.

Figure 4.7: Vermont Maple Special Sugar Train with George Cary center reaching up and Gertrude Franklin the women in the lower left center of the photo (Burlington Free Press May 24 1926 – Chronicling America website).

train stopped in the major cities of Boston, Worchester, New York, Washington, DC, Philadelphia, Pittsburg, Buffalo, Cleveland, and Chicago. With Vermont Governor Billings at the helm and newsmen along to report the journey's progress, the train departed for its first run from Burlington in mid-May 1926 for its twelve-day excursion.[153] Notable stops to meet prominent individuals included the Mayor of New York City and a stop at the White House to visit President Calvin Coolidge. Accompanying Cary on the trip were his personal secretary Gertrude Franklin, his daughter Madeline and niece Della Howe (Figure 4.7).[154] In the first year of its run, it concluded the 2500-mile journey in Burlington, Vermont to be greeted by a few thousand well-wishers along with two marching bands.[155]

On the 1929 journey, one of the exhibition rail cars open to visitors and tourists boasted a banner reading "St. Johnsbury, the Maple Sugar Center of the World." The Cary Company and Maple Grove Candies had extensive displays in one of the cars and at each stop, maple syrup, maple sugar cakes, and maple candies were given as gifts to dignitaries that were met along the way. Interestingly, in 1929, the official photographer for the trip was Harry Richardson of Newport.[156]

The train ran in 1926, 1927 and 1929, but due to floods in 1928 it did not run. In 1929, Governor John E. Weeks led the Vermont entourage in their meeting of President Hoover at the White House in Washington, D.C. In one account, it was said that the next morning, President Hoover enjoyed maple syrup on his pancakes".[157]

Highland Label

Taking the name of his farm in North Danville, the Cary Company began to package "Highland" brand maple syrup for sale to the individual consumer in the 1920s. The Highland brand "Pure Maple Sap Syrup" as it was first called, was packaged in small three-ounce individual serving metal cans and in slightly larger one-pint cans, as well as larger gallon cans (Figure 4.8). Into the 1930s and beyond, it was primarily packaged in glass for purchase from a grocery or through mail order. In addition to Highland Pure Maple Syrup packaged in red cans for sale to consumers for home consumption, there was also Cary's Soft Grain Pure Maple Sugar that was packed in similar cans with a blue and yellow label (Figure 4.9).

Figure 4.8: Highland Maple Recipe Booklet (Author's Collection).

Figure 4.9: Cary's Soft Grain Pure Maple Sugar (Author's Collection).

Syrup purchased by the Cary Company in the 1920s was graded into one of four standards established by the company; fancy, commercial No. 1, commercial No. 2, and commercial No. 3. In general, the industry and maple producers were following voluntary federal color standards that corresponded with each of Cary's grades, and all were expected to have a uniform standard density of eleven pounds to the gallon. Syrup that tested below that density was usually accepted by the Cary Company, but at a reduced rate.[158] The fancy and commercial No. 1 grades of Cary would have been used for packaging in cans and bottles for table syrup as well as conversion to sugar. The commercial no. 2 and 3 grades were used almost exclusively for conversion to block sugar for blending and flavoring food and tobacco products. Cary's four grades were essentially the same as what became known as Fancy, Grade A, Grade B, and Grade C in the grading system formally introduced by the Vermont State government in 1929. Hitchcock's survey of 457 Vermont maple producers in 1925 found that of the 66% that sold syrup to wholesale dealers like Cary, 11% of the syrup was fancy, 50% was commercial No. 1, 27% commercial No. 2, and 12% commercial No. 3.[159]

Print advertising for maple syrup was still in its infancy in the 19-teens and early 1920s, although one did see the occasional magazine advertisement suggesting maple syrup was excellent served on pancakes, and waffles, as well as on ice cream. A new form of informative advertising was beginning to appear from larger regional and national food labels in the form of recipe booklets.

As the Cary Company moved into greater sales for home consumption with their Highland label, they also hopped on this bandwagon. To assist with the promotion of their new label they began printing small illustrated recipe booklets and pamphlets that contained a variety of suggestions for new ways to cook and bake with pure maple syrup (Figures 4:10 and 4.11).

Figure 4.10: Cover of Cary Maple Sugar Company promotional Highland recipe booklet (Author's Collection).

Figure 4.11: Additional examples of Highland Maple Recipe Booklets (Author's Collection).

Vermont Maple Sugar Company and Vermont Maple Syrup Company

Although not a great deal is known about these ancillary companies, Cary was one of the owners of a few other maple ventures in Vermont. One was the Vermont Maple Sugar Company which established a plant at Essex Junction, Vermont in the summer of 1919.[160] Similarly, in June of 1922, George Cary was involved in the creation of another maple corporation in St. Johnsbury, when the articles of incorporation were filed for the Vermont Maple Syrup Company with stock of $50,000. The stockholders of this corporation were listed as Harry Wilson of Boston, Gertrude Franklin, Clinton Cary and George Cary.[161] The purpose of this new venture was not stated at the time; however, it is safe to say that the partners in this firm under George Cary's leadership were positioning themselves for the absorption of other failing maple firms and expansion into more corners of the maple business. The Cary Company purchased the equipment of the failed Vermont Maple Syrup Company from the plant in Lowville, New York in January 1929.[162]

New Faces – New Investments

With the growth of the Cary Company and an increasing need for outside capital, Cary brought in new investors in the early 1920s, most notably the addition of M.W. Reed. Hailing from New York City, Reed came into the company after being on the Board of Directors for the American Tobacco Company and having spent years working as the main purchasing agent for what was known as the Tobacco Trusts where he was responsible for securing the purchase of significant volumes of maple sugar from the Cary Company.[163] With his addition as an investor, Reed was elected a member of the Board of Directors in 1922 and took up the position of Treasurer vacated by the death of Frank Cobb. Other members of the Board of Directors of the Cary Company in 1922 in addition to George Cary as President and Reed as Treasurer were H.B. Stewart of Derby, VT as Vice President; J.H. Turner of Beebe, VT; and

C.J. Darling of Oaks Bluff, NY.[164] A few years earlier, on January 1st of 1920 the Cary Company proposed to sell 2,500 shares of preferred stock at a price of $100 for a total of $250,000 that would return seven percent per year.[165]

The Cary Company was not without its bad apples among the workforce. In one instance recalled by George Cary's daughter Madeline, it was discovered in 1929 that a manager in the New York City office of the Cary Company was not entirely truthful or trustworthy. Madeline herself was then employed in the New York office and with the assistance of her brother Clinton Cary, traveled over the weekend by train from St. Johnsbury to New York City. Arriving on Sunday, they immediately arranged to have the locks changed and on Monday morning as the office opened, presented the outgoing manager with his pink slip and a final check. Harold Whaley was moved into the position to replace the outgoing manager, a move that forever solidified Whaley's connection to the Cary Company and the maple sugar business as will be seen in later chapters.[166]

Maple Grove Candies Enters the Fold

In March 1929, under George Cary's leadership, the Cary Maple Sugar Company partnered with H. Earl Franklin to buy out Katherine Ide Gray and the other stockholders in Maple Grove Candies, Incorporated. With Earl Franklin as President, Gertrude M. Franklin as Vice President, John D. Rickaby as Treasurer and Clinton P. Cary as Clerk, the new Maple Grove Candies, Incorporated began with a capitalization of $100,000.[167] Earl Franklin was a long-time friend of Cary and at the time was working as a syrup buyer for the Cary Company.

The March 1929 purchase was specifically for the candy manufacturing business and did not include Maple Grove Products, Inc. which operated the Maple Grove Inn at the Pinehurst Mansion and the Maple Grove Tea Room in New York City as separate corporate ventures. Katherine Ide Gray and Helen Gray Powell continued in the hospitality business, retaining ownership of Maple Grove Products, Inc.

and continuing to operate these facilities on their own, separate from Maple Grove Candies and the involvement of George Cary or the Cary Maple Sugar Company. It also appears that Ethel McLaren and the investors from Mary Elizabeth Candies were no longer involved with any of the Maple Grove companies following this buyout and splitting of Maple Grove companies.

Gertrude M. Franklin's assumption of the role of Vice President marked an impressive rise through the ranks of the Cary Company that began with her employment as a stenographer for George Cary in April of 1910.[168] Her rise within the company continued as did her personal relationship with George Cary. It was reported that Cary purchased a lot in 1921 on Summer Street for the construction of a home for Franklin, now his personal secretary. The house reportedly had cut-outs of birds in its blue shutters and was named "Birdsacre" in the local directory.[169] In local oral history, and largely unconfirmed, a story is told that Franklin's companionship with George Cary was more than clerical. At one point Franklin was a boarder in the Cary home on Main Street but Mrs. Cary, presumably aware of the close relationship between her husband and Franklin, said that she would not have Franklin living under her roof. In response to this decision, George Cary then built a home for Franklin, presumably the house on Summer Street. A review of the St. Johnsbury directory indicates that in 1909, Gertrude Franklin was a boarder at the Cary house on Main Street. The following year, she was a boarder with a relative on Bagely Street before returning to boarding at the Cary house at 96 ½ Main between 1912 and 1914. In 1916 and 1919 she resided with her brother Earl Franklin at 1 Cary Place, in a house behind the Cary residence, before being listed at the Summer Street home in the 1920s. In 1927 Franklin herself built a new home on Summer Street that she named "Crownlands".[170]

Following the end of the war in 1918 and with an honorable discharge in his hands, Gertrude Franklin's brother, Harold "Earl" Franklin began his employment with the Cary Company (Figure 4.14). Earl Franklin was made-known to George Cary as a local boy and graduate of the St. Johnsbury Academy, but also by the good fortune of being the younger brother of George Cary's personal secretary. Earl Franklin quickly impressed the Cary Company managers and rapidly advanced to become a purchasing agent. Having strong management thinking, Earl Franklin was further invited to join the Cary Company's Board of Directors.[171] Franklin's importance to and close association with George Cary was carried into the role of company President when the Cary Company purchased Maple Grove Candies, Inc. in 1929.

It is unclear what personal financial resources the siblings Gertrude Franklin and Earl Franklin may have brought to the table in being selected as the Vice President and President of Maple Grove Candies during the 1929 purchase. For example, in the case of Gertrude, who came to Cary's attention initially as a company stenographer and then as his personal secretary, one must wonder if her selection for this position was merely as a placeholder for the corporate paperwork. What is clear is that she worked her way through the company to secure George Cary's personal attention and rewards. It is also clear that upon Cary's death and bankruptcy, both Earl Franklin and Gertrude Franklin were removed from their positions on the Board of Maple Grove Candies and their employment with the Cary Company came to an end.

Maple Grove Candies Building
Soon after purchasing Maple Grove Candies, Cary again persuaded the Town of St. Johnsbury to grant him a ten-year tax exemption if he built a new manufacturing plant for Maple Grove Candies.[172] As with the earlier construction of the Cary plant, the town enthusiastically endorsed this proposal.[173] Work began almost immediately on the new brick building, located on Portland Street at the eastern edge of St. Johnsbury, directly in front of the Cary Company plant previously built in 1920 (Figure 4.12).

Figure 4.12: 1929 photo of grand opening of Maple Grove Candies building (Author's Collection).

The new Maple Grove Candies building was originally planned to be a one story building only for the production of maple candy, but plans were modified to add business offices for the Cary Maple Sugar Company and Maple Grove Candies on a second floor. In less than a year the new Maple Grove Candies building was occupied and in full operation (Figure 4.13).

Although separated from the Cary Company plant by the Maine Central Rail Road line, the Maple Grove Candies building was connected to the Cary Company plant by a covered elevated walkway spanning the rail road tracks (Figure 4.14). Technically speaking, Maple Grove Candies was a subsidiary of the Cary Company; however, at the time the Maple Grove Candies building was built, the two companies were viewed by many employees and community members as distinct, but related endeavors.

Figure 4.13: Postcard of Maple Grove Candies building (Author's Collection).

Figure 4.14: Photo of walkway and backside of Maple Grove building as it looks today (photo by author).

Charlie Welcome, a past Maple Grove employee, noted in his written history of the company that "the symbiotic relationship of the two companies was confirmed by an overhead walkway which joined the plants and crossed over the railroad tracks. Some who didn't like Mr. Cary's expansion called the walkway an umbilical cord".[174]

The Cary Company's dominance of the bulk maple sugar and syrup market was undisputed by the middle of the 1920s and had reach a level of control never-before experienced in the maple industry. A 1925 economic survey by the Vermont Agricultural Experiment Station found that of the 457 of Vermont maple syrup producers surveyed, 66% of these farms sold part, or all, of their maple production to wholesale dealers, primarily Cary. Of those 66% farms, 51% of their total maple production went to dealers and 95% of that was in the form of maple syrup.[175] This level of influence had provided the Cary Company with the means to expand their reach and activities beyond the buying and selling of sugar and syrup in the St. Johnsbury area and enter into new areas of the maple industry. Promotion and mass production of the Brower Pipeline System witnessed their entry and involvement in the maple equipment business. The development of their own label, Highland Maple Syrup, for bottling and sale to home consumers was their entry into the specialty foods and the table syrup markets, and their purchase of Maple Grove Candies added the largest maple candy company in the country to their portfolio.

George Cary and the company also took advantage of many of the new opportunities to promote the company and its products, making use of silent film to be shown as early advertisements before feature films in movie houses, mailing out thousands of color-illustrated recipe booklets, and taking part in the annual Maple Sugar Train across the United States promoting Vermont's finest and most famous products. By the end of the 1920s George Cary and the Cary Maple Sugar Company had reached the apex of their industry.

5

The King is Dead

All empires must eventually fall, and Cary's empire was no different. Despite years of growth and development, the company's methods of using credit to float their capital each year was no longer sustainable. Following the stock market crash in the fall of 1929, banks and creditors began to tighten their lending practices. The Cary Company was not immune from the effects of this financial crisis. In 1929 alone, the company faced significant expenses related to the purchase of Maple Grove Candies along with the construction of the Maple Grove building in St. Johnsbury and the Cary Company plant in Lennoxville, Quebec. These expenses, coupled with a threat of increased tariffs on maple sugar coming from Canada and a disagreement in pricing with Cary's largest customer, spelled financial doom for George Cary and the Cary Company. In the midst of the Great Depression, the American Tobacco company demanded a lower price for the purchase of block maple sugar, which the Cary Company refused. American Tobacco in turn chose to buy its sugar elsewhere and the Cary Company found itself with a surplus of millions of pounds of maple sugar, which as essentially a year's supply. With depression-era creditors providing very little room to delay payments, the Cary Company was left without much working capital and a mounting list of bills to pay. By 1931 the company became so far overextended it could not recover.

Without question the Cary Company had become huge by maple industry standards. In a 1929 speech by Clinton Cary to the St. Johnsbury Rotary Club, he reported that the company was employing over 200 people in the United States and Canada and that figure did not include the hundreds of local buying agents they retained in the maple producing areas.[176] In addition, the company had two large plants, one in Lennoxville and one in St. Johnsbury. They had added the Maple Grove Candies Company to their portfolio and had expanded into the hospitality business, operating the Maple Cabin Inn and Maple Cabin Tea Room adjacent to the St. Johnsbury plant. See Figures 5.1 and 5.2 for illustrations of the full extent of the Cary Company complex in St. Johnsbury at that time.

With the addition of the Highland Maple Syrup and Maple Sugar label for home consumption, the company was maintaining warehouses in strategic locations around the country to supply their retail sellers. Such locations included New York City, Chicago, Salt Lake City, Seattle, Portland, Phoenix, Los Angeles, and San Francisco.[177]

In working his way to the top of the industry, Cary encountered detractors and competitors challenging his model and attempting to provide an alternative to doing business with the Cary Company. In some cases, he partnered with the competitors, in and others he simply bought them outright, minimizing his risks. In other cases, he was forced to adjust and respond with changes in pricing and payments as well as changes in how the product was handled and processed on the ground in the United States and Canada, particularly Quebec.

By 1929 the company had a capitalization of $3 million.[178] Since the Cary Company's beginning, each year the Cary Company had obtained substantial short-term loans, personally endorsed by George Cary himself. This was necessary to make available the enormous volumes of cash needed each spring to purchase maple sugar from the farmers through Cary's army of buyers and representatives.

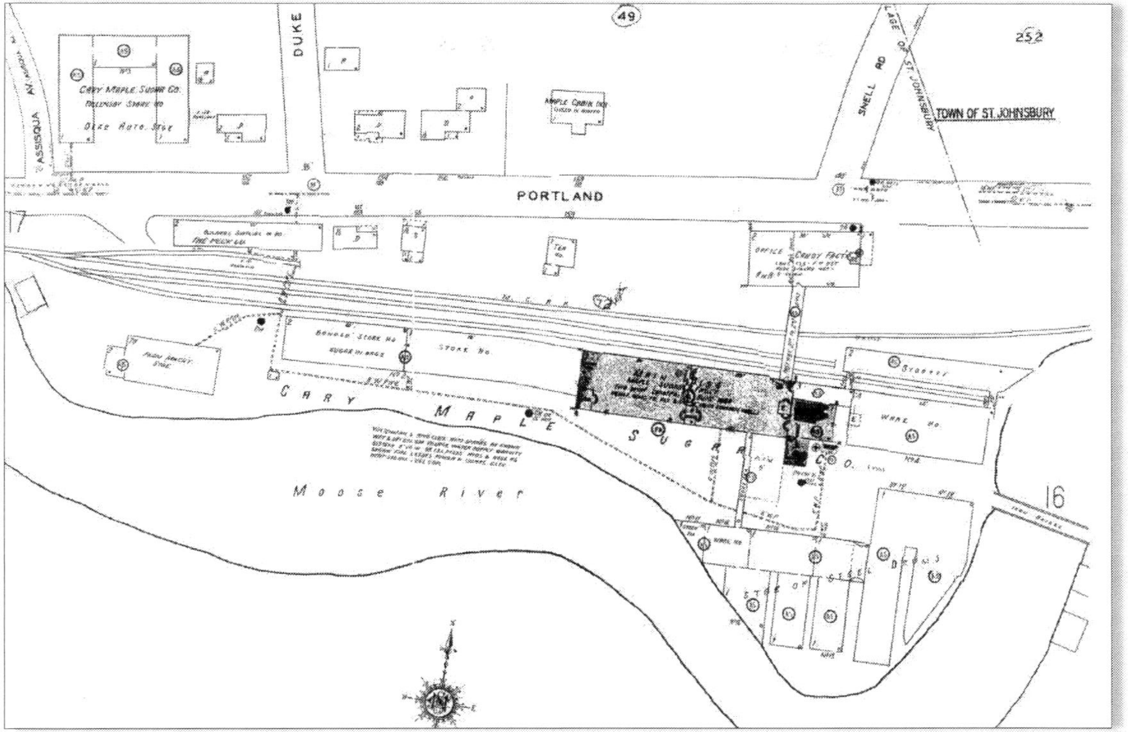

Figure 5.1: 1927-1943 Sanborn fire insurance map showing extent of Cary Company facilities in St. Johnsbury including Cary Plant, Maple Grove Building connected by walkway over railroad tracks, associated warehouses, Maple Cabin Tea Room, and Maple Inn Guest House (Courtesy of Library of Congress).

Figure 5.2: Oblique aerial photo ca. ate 1930s showing full extent of Cary Company complex (Smith 1937 – St. Johnsbury Sesqui-Centennial Program, Author's Collection).

Just in Vermont alone, in 1929 the cash payments to farmers were around $2 million.[179] From 1928 to 1930, the Cary Company faced three years of above average production in the sugarbush and held true to its commitment to pay sugarmakers for syrup it had agreed to purchase despite a surplus and plunging syrup prices.

The Rise of the Maple Cooperatives
Government guides, pamphlets, and articles about operating a sugarbush and the manufacturing of maple sugar and syrup were fairly common in the late nineteenth and early twentieth centuries. These guides presented useful advice and direction on forest management and producing the best grades and quality of maple syrup and sugar. However, absent from these early guides was any mention of marketing. Farmers were left to their own devices. By and large, the better-quality sugar was packed in wooden tubs and the better-quality syrup packaged in one-gallon metal containers, and was sold directly to consumers, shopkeepers and dealers. The remainder of the sugar was retained for home consumption. George Cary came along and presented the maple producer with a new outlet for their sugar and syrups.

These producers were farmers, not salesmen, and Cary's enterprise was a welcome new market and opportunity to more easily sell one's maple products wholesale to a single cash-paying buyer. Producers could avoid dealing with direct sales to consumers and the burdens of unloading their sugar and syrup piecemeal. Maple producers enjoyed this development in their farm business, but not indefinitely. In time producers began to feel that Cary and the other large packers were not giving them a fair price, or at least a price that reflected the cost of making their products. Into the 1920s, maple production guides contained language that was rather disparaging towards packers and buyers of maple syrup and sugar. There was an implication that producers were pure and noble, and the packers were selfish parasites who engaged in blending and adulterating otherwise pure maple syrup. A number of maple cooperatives were born by building on this anti-packer sentiment and wanting a greater piece of the successes they were seeing with the Cary Company.

Clinton Cary addressed the topic of a newly formed maple producers' cooperative at the annual meeting of the National Canners Association in 1922. Clinton noted that a group of maple producers had met in Burlington to form a cooperative marketing association with the intent of promoting and facilitating sales of high quality maple products directly to consumers. While the seeds of the organization were planted, it was Cary's opinion that the meeting was less than successful and that farmers were concerned that in contracting to have their goods sold through the cooperative they lost the freedom to sell whenever, wherever, and to whomever that they had previously enjoyed.[180]

As creators of pure maple syrup, for many producers it was anathema to their interests to produce lower quality maple syrup or sugar that then might be used in making blended cane and maple syrup, a product against which they were directly competing for consumers. In that vein, the Vermont Maple Producers Cooperative Exchange, Inc. was specifically focused on "developing markets and stimulating demand for pure maple syrup and sugar".[181] The Vermont Cooperative was not happy with the uniform price offered for block sugar regardless of quality and instead encouraged farmers to make maple syrup and offer payment at different rates depending on four color grades.[182] A warehouse was established in 1922 in Essex Junction, metal barrels were rented from the Cary Company, and the newly formed Vermont Maple Producers Cooperative Exchange solicited the participation of Vermont sugarmakers.[183] Unfortunately, the cooperative was undercapitalized from the very start and was never able to generate enough interest in their shared vision to reach a volume sufficient to cover their overhead and start-up expenses. The leadership of the Vermont Cooperative later acknowledged that they were warned from the start that it would take more money than they had anticipated to be successful. Cooperative Manager Amos J. Eaton reported in 1926 that "our first mistake as I see it was when we did not realize how much capital would be needed to handle a maple syrup business. Before this organization was started a good many different people were consulted, among them Mr. Cary and he very frankly stated his opinion that this organization could not succeed because no one connected with it had sufficient money to make it successful."[184] To what degree the independent nature of the Vermont farmer dissuaded producers from becoming cooperative members is hard to say, but it certainly cannot be ignored. Rural Vermonters were long known for avoiding what they perceived as a handout and wanting to make a go of things on their own.

With the Vermont Cooperative floundering, one speaker at the annual meeting of the State Sugarmakers commented, "I wonder if the farmers of Vermont appreciate what Mr. Carey (sic) has done for them by way of developing a quantity market for Vermont maple products. I want to say to you if it were not for Carey and some others, the consumption of maple products would not be what it is today. He has developed a quantity market that has been of untold benefit to the farmer." This same speaker went on to extoll the virtues of cooperative marketing and further comment on how great it would be if the "business interests of the Carey Maple Sugar company could be transformed into a cooperative marketing corporation owned and controlled largely by the farmers of Vermont, but managed by just such a genius as George C. Carey."[185] Obviously, that was not in the best interest of the Cary Company and the company did not become a partner in the Vermont Maple Cooperative. The relationship between George Cary and the Vermont Cooperative was never particularly friendly, and it deteriorated further when editors of the Burlington Free Press elected to enter the discussion in defense of the Cooperative Exchange. Cary was put on the defensive and a fascinating series of lengthy back and forth exchanges appeared in the *Burlington Free Press* in February and March of 1929.[186] In the end, the Vermont Maple Products Cooperative was on its way to bankruptcy and its Essex Junction equipment and remaining products were later purchased by the Cary Company.[187]

The Vermont Cooperative Exchange learned the hard way that the success of the Cary Company did not come without risks. Instead, many producers enjoyed the development and growth of the bulk market by the Cary Company and assumed that they could replicate it or even improve upon it with little effort or little risk of their own. In focusing their attention on getting a fair price for their syrup based on quality or grades, producers in the cooperatives worked hard to make as much fancy grade syrup as they could, which would in turn return the best price. However, the cooperative managers soon realized that the light color and delicate flavor of fancy grade maple syrup, which may be perceived as a superior product by the producers, was not as desirable by general consumers. Rather, fancy grade syrup was much more difficult to market and sell than a lower valued, darker grade syrup, with a stronger maple flavor. When the Vermont Maple Cooperative failed to get off the ground, Cary was there to buy up their remaining products and equipment and welcome the producers back into his realm. Although they were able to force an increase in the price paid for syrup by Cary, the Vermont Cooperative was still unable to compete or attract sufficient membership to survive and eventually folded in 1927.[188]

In Quebec, a similar, albeit, more successful, cooperative effort began with the assistance and leadership of the Ministry of Agriculture's maple specialist, Cyrille Vaillancourt. Producers in Quebec were unhappy, feeling that they were at the mercy of the buyers for the maple wholesalers who were offering what they felt was a less than fair price of as low as four to five cents a pound on "take it or leave it" terms. In 1925 in Quebec, 102 maple producers under the guidance of Vaillancourt formed a cooperative called "Les Producteurs de Sucre d'érable du Québec." It was no secret that the Cary Company was the primary wholesaler this new cooperative was working against, or at least hoping to change.[189]

Vaillancourt himself tells a story, recounted in his biography, of traveling from Quebec to St. Johnsbury in early 1925 with a Deputy Minister of Agriculture to visit George Cary and ask him why he pays the same price for maple products regardless of quality. Vaillancourt pressed him with an appeal that better quality sugar deserves a better price. As Vaillancourt tells it, Cary was not to be swayed and replied that he knew his business and was not going to change his ways. Unbeknownst and to the surprise of the higher-ranking Deputy Minister, Vaillancourt spontaneously responded to Cary, that in that case, the Quebec producers would form a cooperative to help producers sell and market their products and obtain a fair price. Which in turn reportedly elicited a response from Cary that, "your cooperative will not survive, and just like the cooperative they attempted to form in Vermont that went bankrupt, you will be glad to see me again and you will return to selling your products to me."[190]

With Vaillancourt as their manager, the Quebec cooperative grew rapidly, increasing from 102 members in 1925, to 1,240 members in 1928, and to over 2,000 in 1931. By working together, the cooperative was successful in finding new markets, notably in the United States, and demanding better prices for the member's products. In time the organization evolved to become today's influential 2,700-member strong Citadelle Maple Syrup Producers Cooperative. It is interesting to note in the modern telling of the history of Citadelle how George Cary is portrayed as the monopolizing villain that was challenged and vanquished by their hero Vaillancourt, which led to the creation and success of the Citadelle Maple Syrup Producers Cooperative.[191]

Although one cooperative survived and the other failed, it does appear to be true that both the Vermont and the Quebec cooperatives were successful in forcing Cary to raise the price he paid for maple syrup. One author, in arguing for the success of the Vermont cooperative, reported that in 1922 the price for a gallon of syrup was about eighty cents, whereas five years later the price had risen to between $1.25 and $1.65 a gallon, depending on the grade.[192] Cary himself was reported to have acknowledged the influence of the Vermont cooperative in stating, "you fellows left me no choice in the matter, you compelled me to raise the price."[193]

Tariff Issues

The issue of tariffs and duties on imports of maple sugar and maple syrup from Canada to the United States was making headlines in the 1920s in the maple producing regions. As the world's largest dealer in maple sugar and syrup, George Cary was frequently asked, and more than happy to share, his opinion on the state of affairs of the industry and proposed tariff changes. Frequent adjustments to the tariff on imports of maple sugar and syrup were a concern for Cary due to his program of purchasing and importing large volumes of sugar from Quebec. While he was quoted as supporting the idea of a tariff to equalize pricing for American producers, Cary was also focused on maximizing his profit and minimizing his costs. In fact, in September of 1924, the Cary Company formally requested a federal investigation of the maple sugar and maple syrup tariffs, which were then set at four cents per pound each for maple syrup and sugar by the Tariff Act of 1922.[194]

Overall, in the 1920s, total syrup and sugar production in the United States was at a greater level than in Canada. But long-term production levels were on the rise in Canada and at the same time were beginning to shrink in the United States, which concerned producers and buyers in the United States.[195] With the Tariff Act of 1922, a tariff was in place whereby Canadian producers were required to pay four cents a pound on syrup and four cents a pound on maple sugar that they were selling to buyers in the United States. Such buyers might be wholesale dealers and packers, local storekeepers, cooperatives, or direct consumers. The purpose of the tariff was reportedly to allow American producers an equal or better chance at selling their products in the United States when put up against what were believed to be lower priced Canadian maple products. The idea was that the tariff would be set at an amount such that it would put the Canadian product at the same price point as the American product when sold in the United States. American producers further argued that the Canadian government was unfairly aiding and subsidizing Canadian maple production, thus providing Canadian producers with an unfair advantage. It was felt that the increasing Canadian production levels were a direct result of Canadian government assistance at a time when U.S. production was shrinking.[196]

Having the tariff set at four cents per pound for both sugar and syrup was problematic because maple sugar and maple syrup were not equivalent pound for pound. It simply cost more to make sugar than syrup. If one was trying to have parity in setting tariff rates, one should account for the fact that the value of maple sugar should also include the value of first producing maple syrup. Producing maple sugar required one reduce the maple sap to level of syrup and then further reduce the water content, taking the syrup down to sugar. What was also not considered in the existing one-size-fits-all tariff were the different values for the various grades of syrup or sugar.

Having the tariff for sugar the same as the syrup tariff at only four cents without considering that it cost more to make maple sugar than syrup was a huge advantage and tariff savings on maple sugar which subsequently encouraged the buying and importing of sugar over syrup by the American wholesale packers. It was no surprise that in the 1920s Canadian imports of maple products were overwhelmingly maple sugar, even though under the lead of the Cary Company, the wholesale maple industry in the United States had begun a shift to selling and buying syrup in barrels. As discussed earlier, the Cary Company had been moving away from the purchase of block sugar and wanted to focus their buying exclusively on maple syrup. They could then convert the syrup to sugar in their plants under their direction and quality controls. With the disparity in tariff pricing it was more cost effective to take advantage of the lower tariff for sugar.[197]

Further wading into this issue, in January of 1929 at a hearing before the House Ways and Means Committee in Washington, D.C. George Cary testified on issues related to raising the tariff on maple products. Despite being a large buyer of Canadian maple sugar, Cary supported the tariff and suggested that it be raised to six cents a pound on syrup and ten cents a pound on sugar.[198] The following year President Hoover passed the Hawley-Smoot Tariff Bill raising the tariff on maple syrup to 5.5 cents and 8 cents for maple sugar.

By late 1929 it was understood that the tariff rate on maple sugar was going to be doubled from 4 to 8 cents beginning in middle of 1930. In response, American wholesale maple dealers began to purchase as much Quebec maple sugar as they could lay their hands on, with the Cary Company being a key participant in this buying frenzy. However, as noted above, producers with the new Quebec cooperative were holding onto their sugar in hopes that prices would rebound. It was reported in November 1930 that the Cary Company had nearly 15 million pounds of maple sugar on hand.[199] As will be seen, sitting on top of this enormous surplus of sugar, equal to the amount the St. Johnsbury plant normally processed in single year, was going to come back to haunt the Cary Company.

As a side note, the tariff on maple syrup and sugar was reduced in 1936 and continued to shrink through the 1930s and 1940s before eventually being abandoned entirely. In the current era of the 21st century, the price of syrup is controlled on a global scale by a small number of major buyers and packers in Canada and the United States and today the market of syrup is much more stable due to the strategic syrup reserves in Quebec.[200]

Figure 5.3: Backside of Cary factory with stockpile of metal drums along Moose River (Courtesy of Tom Olson and New England Maple Museum).

Loss of an Ally

In 1930, the Cary Company was reported to have 15 million pounds of maple sugar on hand which was estimated to amount to a complete year's supply of what was normally purchased. This massive surplus was believed at the time to be driving down the price of sugar in the United States and Canada. Recognizing that such a surplus was available and that maple sugar prices on the market were notably lower than in the recent past, the American Tobacco Company, the Cary Company's largest client, was expecting to see a concomitant drop in the price they were going to pay for sugar. However, Cary didn't lower his pricing and to Cary's surprise, the American Tobacco Company held strong and refused to pay the price being asked by the Cary Company.[201] As discussed earlier, the American Tobacco Company was a key component to the business model of the Cary Company. In one sense, one could argue that it was the partnership with the tobacco company that led to the creation of the Cary Company in the first place, and to the success that Cary had achieved thus far.

To Cary, the idea of losing the American Tobacco Company must have seemed beyond possibility. The Cary Company gambled and didn't budge on their price. Unfortunately, they misjudged the tobacco company, who wouldn't give in either, and instead choose to take their business elsewhere. Cary was left sitting on millions of pounds of sugar with no one to sell it to and now experiencing a significant cut in revenue. Figure 5.3 illustrates the enormous stockpile of maple syrup that was often on hand at the Cary plant in St. Johnsbury. Reportedly, it was necessary in the following year for the Cary Company to convert this surplus of block sugar back into maple syrup to be able to sell it.[202]

Bankruptcy

During the Great Depression, credit became more and more difficult to acquire, even for successful, seemingly solvent businesses, such as the Cary Company. Cary faced a tightening of financial markets and the inability to secure loans and credit to pay producers as he had always done. Creditors were less willing to make arrangements with debtors to repay their loans. Instead they were demanding repayment in full, or on a short turn-around which was nearly impossible. For many years Cary had signed on many of the company's loans with a personal guarantee that kept the company running year to year, as opposed to simply representing the company and the board when negotiating with creditors. Unfortunately, when the loans went into default, it was Cary himself who then became personally liable rather than the company.

To make matters worse, George Cary's health was in serious decline. It is hard to say precisely to what degree George Cary's failing health affected his ability to work. At the end of the 1920s he was not well and getting worse. It is likely that he found it more and more difficult to attend to his business sun up to sun down as he had in the past, not to mention the growing stress of being unable to repay his loans at a time when the scale of the company had never been greater. According to the Cary family, the advanced state of George's illness by 1931 made it impossible to personally travel to New York City to meet with the company's creditors and lenders to secure the needed funds to pay for the annual springtime expenses, including the usual large amounts of cash needed by his buyers to pay their thousands of producers.[203]

In July of 1931 Cary admitted that he was no longer physically able to run the company and by August of that year had resigned as President. At that same time, his son Clinton Cary also left the company, resigning from the Board of Directors, as did George's close associate Earl Franklin. Leadership of the company was then placed in the hands of bankers Perley F. Hazen and Gilbert E. Woods. Robert M. Boright was brought from his position with the Cary Company in Lennoxville, Quebec to serve as company president and manage the plant operations in St. Johnsbury.[204]

Because Cary's personal finances were so interwoven with those of the Cary Company and Maple Grove Candies, when the American Tobacco Company was unwilling to accept the prices Cary was offering, and the creditors demanding payment on their loans, George Cary's personal assets were decimated. In mid-September shortly after his resignation, George Cary was forced to declare personal bankruptcy. George Cary's estate and the homes, farms, animal stock, sugarbushes, and many acres of land were sold at auction in early November. The Cary Company and its subsidiary, Maple Grove Candies, continued to operate with new leadership and a new board of directors essentially chosen by their largest creditors. In discussing the situation and its effects on the Cary Company, new company President Robert Boright told the Burlington Free Press "Mr. Cary of course, has never had in my opinion, personal worth equal to the amount of his accommodation endorsements, and I doubt very much whether any serious reliance has ever been placed upon the financial value of such endorsements."[205]

Figure 5.4: Post-bankruptcy poster for auction of Cary estate (Courtesy of the Fairbanks Museum and Planetarium).

Papers for George Cary's personal bankruptcy were filed on September 19, 1931 with debts totaling $3,221,046.37 and assets amounting to $101,101.88. At the time this was the second largest bankruptcy filing in the State of Vermont. This bankruptcy was for Cary personally, and not the Cary Maple Sugar Company or Maple Grove Candies. The overwhelming portion of the debt, over $2.8 million, was for loans Cary signed off on for the Cary Company and Maple Grove Candies. Banks and trust companies in New York City and Montreal were the largest providers of credit left with unpaid notes, totaling many hundreds of thousands of dollars.[206] A bankruptcy auction sale held on November 4, 1931 for Cary's Highland Farm in North Danville attracted over 2000 people (Figure 5.4).

Death of the Maple King

Suffering from the stress of losing everything and the company he built from nothing, and with his health continuing to fail, seventeen days after the sale of his Highland farm, George Clinton Cary died on November 21, 1931 at his St. Johnsbury home. He was 67 years old. Cary's doctor determined that he suffered from Bright's disease with his death certificate indicated he died of interstitial nephritis, a chronic kidney disorder leading to long-term kidney damage and ultimately, kidney failure. As a notable leader in the St. Johnsbury community, the Caledonian newspaper noted that all work in the village stopped on the afternoon of Cary's funeral.

Settlement of the bankruptcy continued after Cary's death and was at times slow going due to the complicated nature of many of Cary's property holdings. In the "Trustee's Final Report and Account" for Cary's bankruptcy proceedings, Trustee W. Arthur Simpson reported that "the titles of practically every parcel of real estate and a portion of the personal property were in dispute."[207] For example Cary held joint ownership of numerous parcels of land with Gertrude M. Franklin, his one-time personal secretary and later business partner and eventual vice-president of Maple Grove Candies. Of note, Cary and Franklin together owned equal shares in a large portion of the land encompassing the undeveloped grounds of the Pinehurst Mansion.

The business relationship and the nature of the partnership between Cary and Franklin was certainly one of great trust and closeness. In fact, in the records of Cary's bankruptcy, one finds mention that Gertrude Franklin was the named benefactor of a $5000 life insurance policy carried by George Cary. Unfortunately for Gertrude Franklin, Cary had taken out a loan on the policy for an unstated amount of money, thus reducing the value paid to Franklin.[208]

The most difficult aspect of the bankruptcy proceedings to be settled was the issue of the debts and un-paid notes that Cary has signed for the Cary Maple Sugar Company and its subsidiaries. As expected, the banks and trusts that made these loans filed claims, intending to recover the outstanding debt. However, Trustee Simpson pointed out that if the claims were judged in the favor of the lenders, and the Cary Company itself was forced to repay these notes, then company would be forced into bankruptcy itself and the process would result in years of negotiations that may ultimately prove futile. The majority of Cary's wealth at the time of bankruptcy was in the stock of the Cary Maple Sugar Company and would have been worth many hundreds of thousands of dollars had the company been solvent. Unfortunately, the effects of the bankruptcy on the value of the company rendered the Cary Company stock worthless. Trustee Simpson instead proposed a series of stipulations combined with signed releases, ultimately leading to a surrendering of all the claims by the banks.[209]

Following the family bankruptcy and the death of her husband, Annie Cary and her parents, who lived in the Main Street house along with the Cary family, were graciously allowed to remain in their beautiful home for a few more years while several the other rooms in the house were also rented out. In 1933 the new owner of the house, a Mr. Graham, decided to divide it into three apartments leading Annie Cary, daughter Ruth and her parents to vacate the house and move a short distance north to a smaller home at 114 Main Street. With the death of Annie's father, Joseph Partridge, in 1935 from complications related to gangrene in his foot, she and her mother again relocated to an apartment a few doors away at 104 Main Street, always staying close to their original home at 102 Main Street.

Annie Mae Cary remained in St. Johnsbury with her mother until their deaths a few short weeks apart in 1945. Annie Mae passed away from a heart attack related to hypertension and arteriosclerosis on May

7th at age 71, and her mother Emma Partridge passed on May 28th at age 90.[210]

Like the rest of the Cary assets, the Highland Farm and its surrounding woods and sugarbush were sold as a part of Cary's bankruptcy proceedings. The portion of the sugarbush that was formerly a part of the Waterman's farm, including the sugarhouse, was initially purchased from Cary by a man named Marshall, who in turn sold it back to the Waterman family in 1943 or 1944.

Figure 5.5: Cary Maple Sugar Company lettering still visible on side of Waterman sugarhouse, 2003 (photo by author).

It has remained in the ownership of the Waterman family ever since; however, the maple woods and sugarhouse went unused for many years following Cary's demise. It wasn't until 1989, when Joe Newell and Molly (Waterman) Newell, the family's most recent owners of the farm, began to tap the woods and make maple syrup again, an activity which continued into the early 2000s.[211] While not presently being used to boil sap, the Waterman's sugarhouse is still standing and retains the same red walls and white trim appearance from the early twentieth century (Figure 5.5).

The Stanton sugarhouse, located next to the Waterman sugarhouse in the maple woods at the former Highland Farm also went through a change in hands. Likewise, with the Cary bankruptcy, this sugarhouse and portion of the woods were put up for sale; however, unlike the Waterman family at the time, the Stanton family felt that they couldn't afford to buy it back. Waterman family history tells the story that Stephen Waterman wanted to see the woods stay with their neighbors and offered to help the Stanton's regain their farm. Being a family of some means, the Waterman family offered to loan the Stanton family the money to purchase the woods and sugarhouse, which the Stanton family accepted.[212] The Stanton family later sold the farm and woods in the 1950s and the sugarbush was left idle for twenty years, until 1972, when the Stanley Jones family purchased the maple woods without knowing the history of George Cary or his connection to the land. Stanley Jones came to the area from Ohio and bought the woods specifically to run a sugarbush, having been told that in the past that these woods produced some very good syrup.

Figure 5.6: Cary log cabin built for silent film in 1927 and still standing in Jones Sugarbush in North Danville (photo by author).

Until recently, Stanley Jones' son Stephen Jones and his wife Diane carried on the tradition, making syrup from 4,000 taps at their Sugar Ridge Farm.[213] Over time Stephen Jones learned about George Cary and his role in maple history and the history of St. Johnsbury and North Danville. More importantly, Jones came to recognize the significance and history of his sugarbush, prompting him to make an extra effort to preserve and protect the buildings Cary left behind. Jones has worked to stabilize and preserve the still standing log cabin Cary built on the site that appears in the silent film from the 1920s (Figure 5.6). The Jones' continue to maintain the sugarhouse in the appearance of the Cary era, including painting it the same bright barn red with white trim.

The Cary Company arguably reached its zenith in 1929, at which time a combination of financial challenges, both self-made and external, worked together to bring about a catastrophic collapse of the company. Years of success had encouraged the company to expand and take on additional assets, such as the construction of a new plant in Quebec, and the purchase of Maple Grove Candies, and construction of another new facility in St. Johnsbury. Unfortunately, these were undertaken at time in the nation's financial history when working with creditors was increasingly risky. On top of that, changes in tariff rates led to a run on maple sugar from Quebec, leading the Cary Company to have greater expenses and unplanned surpluses than ever before in a landscape of tighter than ever terms from the banks and lenders. Not expecting a change in their long-standing partnership, the Cary Company was caught off guard when then tobacco industry clients demanded a reduction in the price of maple sugar.

Greater than ever operating expenses, a year's supply of product on their hands with no one to sell it to, a greatly diminished ability to get loans and credit, coupled with the risky practice of personal endorsement on company lending, ultimately resulted in the personal bankruptcy of George Cary. The Cary Company was not insulated from the effects of George Cary's bankruptcy and was taken into receivership by their largest creditors. Sadly, George Cary's poor health worsened and carried him into death. However, as much as George Cary's demise shocked the maple industry, the village of St. Johnsbury, and his maple empire company, it did not lead to the death of the Cary Maple Sugar Company.

6

A New Empire in a New Era

New Owners – New Directions

George Cary's resignation prior to his bankruptcy and death resulted in a change in company leadership and the installation of Robert Boright as plant manager and temporary president. However, Boright's position was simply as a placeholder, and when the dust settled from the bankruptcy, Boright purchased the Cary plant in Quebec and returned to Lennoxville. At the direction of the controlling financiers, The Fidelity Trust Company, Preston Herbert took Boright's place as company President and Edward R. Boylan was installed as Vice President.[214]

Herbert came to his position with the Cary Company though his many years of involvement with the tobacco industry, including a stint as head of the tobacco section of the Quartermasters Corps for the United States Army during World War I. Herbert later assumed employment with the American Tobacco Company, where he rose to the level of an executive before retiring to his farm at Briarcliff Manor, Georgia. Having shown previous success at reorganizing a large tobacco export company, Herbert was drawn out of retirement to assist with the reorganization of the Cary Company and its subsidiaries following George Cary's bankruptcy and the company being taken into receivership.[215]

As President, Herbert was not known for being what might be called a "people person" and left much of the day-to-day management of the company and the employees to his Vice President, Edward Boylan. Herbert traveled frequently around the country on business for the company and when he could get away, he continued to spend time with his wife and family who remained at their Georgia farm.[216] Instead of taking the spotlight himself, Herbert handled the bigger financial issues behind the scenes. He recognized Boylan's knack for advertising, marketing, and managing people and gave Boylan a great deal of freedom to direct day-to-day activities as he saw fit.[217]

In his unpublished history of the Cary Company, Charlie Welcome remembers Herbert as something of a recluse when he was in St. Johnsbury, living alone with his bulldog in the Moore Hotel on Railroad Street. Coming from the southern United States and the business world of New York City, Herbert's sense of fashion, namely spats and a Derby, was out of place in the northeast Kingdom of Vermont in the 1930s and was most certainly noticed as he walked to and from work on Portland Street every day.[218]

Like with Herbert, the selection of Edward Boylan for the position of Vice President may have been somewhat strategic and made to protect the interests of the tobacco companies. Boylan was the son of Richard J. Boylan, the Vice President of the American Tobacco Company in charge of purchasing. Leaving their 1929 disagreement over prices behind them, the American Tobacco Company had renewed its relationship with the Cary Company as the Company's largest client.[219] With his new position, Edward Boylan purchased a home and moved his family from New York City to St. Johnsbury where they remained until the Cary Maple Sugar Company was sold in 1953.[220]

Bankruptcy and receivership didn't just bring new names and faces to the helm at the Cary Company; it also resulted in change for a handful of key personnel, some only temporarily and some permanently. As noted earlier, with his father's resignation Clinton Cary also left his position with the Cary Company and found work with former Cary Company Vice President John Rickaby. Rickaby at that time was operating another maple sugar company in Essex Junction, Vermont, and welcomed Clinton Cary's expertise. However, a few years later with the Cary Company reorganized and under receivership, Clinton Cary accepted an invitation to rejoin the company as a Vice President, where he continued to work until he contracted pneumonia in the winter of 1935-1936 and unexpectedly died at the young age of 37.[221] Like her older brother, daughter Ruth Cary returned to work for the company for a short while following the death of her father, accepting employment as a stenographer in 1933.

With the difficulties of the Cary Company and Maple Grove Candies and the death of her employer and friend George Cary, Gertrude Franklin either willingly stepped down or was removed from her position as Vice President with Maple Grove Candies in 1933. Gertrude Franklin continued to live in St. Johnsbury for a few more years before selling her "Crownlands" home in 1939 and leaving St. Johnsbury. Gertrude eventually settled in New York City before her death in 1976 at age 87.[222]

Like his sister Gertrude, Earl Franklin's tenure with the Cary Company and Maple Grove Candies quickly came to an end with Cary's bankruptcy and the companies going into receivership. However, Earl Franklin's involvement with the maple industry was far from done and he did not move away from St. Johnsbury. For a short period in the 1930s after leaving Maple Grove Candies, Franklin worked for Fairfield Farms Maple Company as a commercial traveler. But in the 1940s he became the President-Treasurer and principal buying agent of maple sugar and syrup for the "Our Husbands Company" out of Lyndon, Vermont, taking on the role of neighborhood competitor to the Cary and Maple Grove Candies companies. The Our Husbands Company specialized in veterinary medicines and patent medicines but also sold canned and bottled syrup under its own label, as well as selling bulk syrup to blenders. Franklin continued to work in this capacity through the 1950s before his death in 1963.[223]

In 1934 the Cary Company was finally able to put the sour taste of bankruptcy and the uncertainty of receivership behind them. At the beginning of the year, as part of the settlement of the bankruptcy and claims against the company, a federal judge ordered that "the entire property of the Cary Maple Sugar Company will be sold at auction to the highest bidder."[224] Because they were unable to separate Cary's personal property from that of the company, the sale included the entirety of Cary's real estate, ranging from Cary's residential dwelling in St. Johnsbury and his farms in Danville, to the warehouses around the state and of course the manufacturing plant and associated buildings in St. Johnsbury. An auction was carried out as planned at the St. Johnsbury plant on January 31st, 1934, and to no one's surprise the corporate assets of the Cary Company, including the physical plant, facilities and brand, were purchased by the newly re-organized Cary Maple Sugar Company.[225]

Figure 6.1: Portrait of Clinton P. Cary not long before his death (Courtesy of Fairbanks Museum and Planetarium).

A few weeks later the Company further announced the election of new officers and board of directors. Preston Herbert continued as President, Clinton Cary came back on board as Vice President and

Treasurer, and four men were named directors, including Arthur Simpson of Lyndonville, who had served as Trustee of the Cary Estate for the bankruptcy, and prominent maple equipment manufacturer, George H. Soule of St. Albans.[226] As an interesting aside, in 1907 George H. Soule was referred to as the "maple sugar king of Vermont" because of his relatively large 7,000 tap maple operation.[227]

Sadly, Clinton Cary's time back with the company was short-lived. As noted earlier, in March of 1937 at the young age of 37 Clinton Cary was unable to recover from a two-week bout of pneumonia and died at the hospital in St. Johnsbury. Clinton Cary was replaced as Vice-President by past Vice-President, Edward Boylan. Like his father before him, the funeral of Clinton was well attended by townsfolks and representatives of the maple industry from Vermont and Quebec.[228]

Maple Grove Candies, the candy making arm of the Maple Grove enterprise that was purchased by the Cary Company in 1929, as discussed in Chapter Four, was also subject to organizational changes with company receivership. Under the tenure of Herbert and Boylan in the 1930s, Maple Grove Candies changed its name to simply Maple Grove, Incorporated, dropping the word "Candies" from its title. Maple Grove continued to do well making and packaging a variety of candies and maple products. By 1937 Maple Grove was reported to be doing more shipping by rail out of St. Johnsbury than any other business in the area, with thousands of orders for their candies and confections going to all corners of the country each year.[229]

Although separated from Maple Grove Candies with the sale of the candy making wing of the company to Cary and Franklin in 1929, the Maple Grove Inn and Tea Room at the Pinehurst Mansion in St. Johnsbury and the Maple Grove Restaurant in New York City continued to be owned and operated by the Gray family through the 1930s. The Maple Grove Restaurant on West 57th Street in New York stayed in operation until 1932 under the management of Helen Gray Powell and her husband Harold Gates Powell. Katherine Ide Gray continued to manage and serve guests at the Maple Grove Inn and Tea Room on

Western Avenue in St. Johnsbury until as late as 1941, although for many years it was listed for sale by the Passumpsic Savings Bank.[230]

In 1944 the nearby St. Johnsbury Academy began leasing the old Maple Grove Inn/Pinehurst Mansion for use as an extra girls' dormitory. A few years later the old estate was sold and put to use as the St. Johnsbury Chapter of the Elks Lodge in 1946.[231] The stately grounds have been modified and reduced in size slightly over the years, but the building continues to retain much of it original exterior architectural design and appearance, which led to it being listed on the National Register of Historic Places as part of the St. Johnsbury Main Street Historic District in 1975. The Elks Lodge continues to occupy the building on Western Avenue to this day.[232]

Over the years with the addition of the Maple Grove Candies building and other ancillary structures, the footprint of the Cary Company complex on Portland Avenue became rather extensive. The final full extent of the St. Johnsbury facilities of the Cary Maple Sugar Company and Maple Grove Candies covered over five acres as can be seen in the aerial photo in Figure 5.2. In the center is the four-story plant with the sign on the roof reading "Cary Maple Sugar Co." Extending to the right of the plant is the long wooden warehouse and to the left an enormous gambrel roofed storage building. Behind the plant along the bend in the Moose River are numerous covered storage facilities. In the center of the image is the newer two-story brick Maple Grove Candies building connected to the plant by the covered elevated walkway over the railroad tracks. In the bottom center of the photo along the curving driveway is the Maple Cabin Tea Room and across from it the Maple Cabin Inn. Lastly, in the upper left adjacent to a bridge across the Moose River is a glimpse of a portion of the Cary saw mill. The ensemble of buildings was later completed with the addition of the Maple Museum Sugarhouse mentioned below. In later years, many of the wooden warehouses and storage buildings were removed or replaced resulting in a somewhat different overall appearance and smaller footprint today.

Shifting the Focus

Into the 1930s and 1940s, the use of maple sugar for the processing of tobacco products by American tobacco companies gradually declined in favor of other methods and products. This was primarily due to occasional shortages and rising costs of maple sugar, although they did not entirely cease to use maple sugar.[233] Tobacco companies continued to purchase a few million pounds of maple sugar a year prior to the beginning of World War II.

The temporary disarray caused by the Cary Company bankruptcy in 1931 resulted in a broader reorganization of the bulk sugar and syrup market, with new companies coming into the mix and substantial growth of existing smaller companies.[234] As a result, the volume of maple syrup handled by the Cary Company shrank and the size and number of contracts for bulk maple sugar were reduced. Production in Quebec was on the rise through the 1930s while in the United States it was in decline, with a severe drop during and shortly after World War II. The Quebec cooperative centered out of Plessisville continued to grow in size and influence, and other previously smaller packers increased their volume and market share, along with new firms that came on the scene. By 1950 there were as many as ten major firms buying or handling syrup between the United States and Canada. Of these, the Cary Company continued to be the largest by volume on the American side of the border but was processing or handling less than half of the volume that was passing through the hands of the Quebec cooperative Le Producteurs de Sucre d'Érable de Quebec.[235] In a 1956 presentation at the "Third Conference on Maple Products" in Philadelphia, Pennsylvania, Boylan noted that of the four major categories of use for maple products, the market for use by the tobacco industry "has virtually been lost," going from many millions of pounds to less than 200,000 pounds.[236]

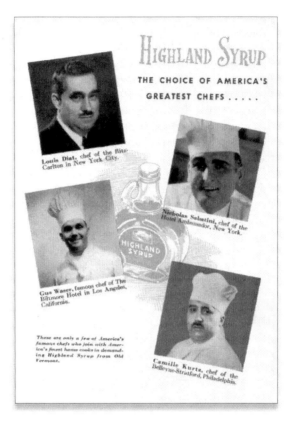

Figure 6.2: Image of famous chef's promoting Highland Maple Syrup in Cary Company promotional booklet (Author's Collection).

In response to this loss, the Cary Company worked to expand existing non-tobacco markets and develop new markets for maple sugar and maple syrup. Company Vice President Boylan addressed this need by greatly increasing the focus on marketing and used advertising and marketing tools not previously employed or utilized by the company. For example, the Cary Company greatly expanded their promotion of the Highland Maple Syrup label and enlisted a series of well-known chefs to endorse the use of Highland syrup with a series of widely distributed recipe booklets (see Figure 6.2).

The Cary Company had dabbled with free recipe booklets and pamphlets in the 1920s, but it was in the later 1930s and 1940s that they expanded the circulation of these promotional items (see also Chapter Four).

Figure 6.3: Advertisement for refillable Highland Syrup bottles (Author's Collection).

    Boylan was tireless in his marketing efforts and even came up with other ways to encourage restaurants and hotels to serve maple syrup to the public including the use of small refillable three-ounce bottles with the Highland Syrup and Cary Pure Maple Syrup labels (Figure 6.3). Instead of buying cans or bottles of syrup in sizes larger than a customer wanted, especially customers less familiar with the flavor of real maple syrup, one could buy a small amount at a time at a store or restaurant and then bring the bottle back to be filled again on a later visit. Unfortunately, the idea never took hold, but one does regularly see the small three-ounce Highland brand syrup bottles for sale today in antique markets.[237]

- MAPLE KING -

Figure 6.4: Cary Company trade show display ca. late 1930s (Courtesy of Maple Grove Farms, Inc.).

Boylan worked with cereal, ice cream, and cookie manufactures to add maple flavored items to their product lines. Boylan himself made appearances on radio shows and television shows and arranged for Highland Syrup to be a sponsor of the children's program "Kukla, Fran, and Ollie".[238] Boylan also attended trade fairs with other Cary Company sales representatives to promote their products with the growing grocery market industry (Figure 6.4).

In the late 1930s, to compete with the major syrup blenders on the market, like Log Cabin and Vermont Maid, the Cary Company began to market their own blended syrup which contained 15% pure maple syrup and 85% cane syrup. Manufacturing and selling blended syrup under their own label was something that had never been done under George Cary's leadership. With the addition of a blended syrup to their product line, Boylan wished to distinguish between the blended and the pure maple syrup by labeling the pure maple syrup "Cary's 100% Pure Maple Syrup" and using the already established Highland label for the blended syrup. This began the use of the name "Cary's" with the apostrophe and "s" after the name Cary as a brand of maple syrup. The Highland syrup label continued in use by the Cary Company up until the company was sold and left St. Johnsbury in 1953, after which time the Highland label was discontinued. The Cary's label however continued in use after this date, as is discussed below.[239]

The Cary Company further diversified their production by providing contracted packaging of syrup and candies under a variety of private labels, notably for high end hotels and gourmet food shops. The Cary Company also expanded their retail brand names for various markets by adding labels for blended syrups they bottled such as *Happy Jack* and *Snow Hugg'd* pancake syrups.[240]

New Ownership

Preston Herbert's position at the helm of the company came to an unexpected end when he died of a heart attack in late November of 1941. In response to his untimely death, the board of directors in 1942 elected existing board member Arthur Simpson as Chairman of the Board and promoted Edward Boylan from Vice President to President.[241] In the following year, the Cary Company was finally out of the ownership and oversight of the banks and creditors that assumed control with receivership. In 1943 a group of New England investors, with the strong financial assistance of Judge Harry Stone of Massachusetts, completed the purchase of the company and its subsidiaries, shifting ownership back to private hands. Leadership of the company continued under Simpson and Boylan with Harold Whaley continuing as plant manager. A notable addition to the board of directors was James Stone of Brockton, Massachusetts, nephew of Judge Harry Stone.[242] The influence of control of the Stone family in the business of the Cary Company continued to grow as was evident in the 1945 election of the board of directors when James Stone became Vice President and his uncles Judge Harry K. Stone and Abraham Stone were added as general board members. Three of the seven members of the board of directors were now from the Stone Family of Boston and Brockton,

Massachusetts; this was a family known elsewhere at the time for their ownership of the Converse Rubber Company and Converse footwear.[243]

The election of a new board in 1945 also saw Edward Boylan replace Arthur Simpson, who stepped down as Company President. The year before Simpson spent much of 1944 campaigning for the position of GOP candidate for governor of Vermont. Sadly, for Simpson, he was soundly defeated in the August primary by then Lieutenant Governor Mortimer R. Proctor, who went on the win the Governorship with 65% of the vote. Simpson continued to seek office and won the seat for state representative for Lyndonville in 1946.

In 1943, during the war years, maple syrup production was down significantly and government controls on pricing and availability of sugar products were in place. Companies were forced to get creative in the face of the limited availability of ingredients and shrunken markets, leading the Cary Company to consider adding apple syrup as a new product line. Apple syrup was used in a variety of products like cosmetics, baby foods, and the processing of cigarette and other tobacco products. The plan never came to be as the apple supply was rather small and the federal government set the price for apples very low to encourage use in other manners, in addition to basic raw consumption by the general-public.[244]

Maple sugar continued to be used in the processing of tobacco for cigarette production during the war years, with cigarettes considered an important item for soldiers and the war effort. This provided the Cary Company with the privilege of being exempted from some of the government restrictions. However, such freedoms were of little help when the supply of maple syrup had dwindled due to many farms discontinuing maple production. Additionally, many of the men from the farms and rural communities had enlisted in the armed forces.

Like with the idea of manufacturing apple syrup, Boylan was known to be open to trying new products and developing new markets. In 1949 Boylan reported that the Cary Company in conjunction with Evans Research and Development Laboratory had developed a new high flavored maple syrup and maple sugar by "capturing the maple essence as the sap is boiled down". Boylan noted that the company planned to share this discovery with the world, although there is no indication that it was ever shared or that it made any noticeable impact on the maple products industry.[245]

Separation of the Cary Maple Sugar Company and Maple Grove

Through the 1930s and early 1940s the Cary Company's corporate owners were very hands off and the Cary Company was largely left in the hands of Preston Herbert and Edward Boylan to be run as they saw fit, and as long as they continued to turn a profit. Even when the Cary Company was reported to have merged with T. Noonan & Sons, Inc. in October 1947 there were no changes planned in the operations or management of the plant in St. Johnsbury.[246] However, Arthur Simpson, now Vermont State Commissioner of Social Welfare, did resign as Chairman of the Board, citing "pressure of other business."[247] T. Noonan & Sons, Inc. was a company that made and sold hair care products and barbershop supplies, for which there was no real connection to the maple or food industries. Rather, this merger was merely a financial investment on the part of the owners of the Cary Company.

However, the purchase of the Cary Company on May 13, 1953 by Natural Sugars, Incorporated, a subsidiary of Fred Fear & Company, Incorporated, was the beginning of significant change for the Cary Company.[248] Early in 1952 in the process of negotiating the sale, Natural Sugars and Fred Fear were reported to be primarily interested in the Cary Maple Sugar Company portion of the business and not the Maple Grove brand or their specialty candy products. In making plans for the purchase, Fred Fear & Company announced that they intended to close the Cary and Maple Grove operations in St. Johnsbury and move the Cary Company equipment to their facilities on the waterfront in Brooklyn, New York. In his position as company President, Edward Boylan was privy to the plans for purchase of the Cary Company and its likely demise as a business in St. Johnsbury. Not wishing to see the St. Johnsbury plant close, Boylan called together plant manager Herbert

Whaley and other prominent employees at the company in St. Johnsbury to inform them of the state of affairs and planned sale. Boylan was especially concerned for the fate of the hundreds of workers, some of whom had been with the company for decades. As was common for the time, most of the workers did not have a pension plan.[249]

Executives at Fred Fear & Company offered Boylan the position of President in the new Cary Company operations in New York, specifically wanting him to assist with the transition, which he ultimately accepted. Unfortunately, they presented no plan or apparent interest in relocating or continuing the Maple Grove products or production line, which was concerning to Boylan. According to Charlie Welcome, the son-in-law of Edward Boylan, Boylan himself seriously considered trying to purchase Maple Grove and keep it operating in St. Johnsbury.

Fortunately for St. Johnsbury and those still employed at Maple Grove, plant manager Herbert Whaley stepped forward with an offer to purchase the Maple Grove portion of the Cary Company. With Whaley's offer, Boylan worked with new owners T. Noonan & Sons and Fred Fear & Company, Inc. to split the companies and sell Maple Grove to Whaley. Boylan further assisted Whaley in securing financing, since the local banks were apprehensive about working with a relatively unknown buyer on such a sizable transaction.[250]

In September 1953 Harold R. Whaley completed the purchase of Maple Grove from Fred Fear & Company of New York and became Maple Grove's new President and sole stockholder. With Whaley's purchase of Maple Grove, he also secured a long-term lease for the use of the two-story Maple Grove building on Portland Street, along with the Maple Cabin and the recently erected Maple Museum. This preserved a future for Maple Grove and maintained St. Johnsbury's connection to their past title as Maple Center of the World.[251]

Figure 6.5: Postcard of the Maple Museum and Maple Cabin at Maple Grove Farms, ca. late 1950s (Author's Collection).

Looking for ways to further catch the attention of passing tourists, Whaley arranged for the construction of a replica of a traditional wood plank sugarhouse complete with a cupola on top (Figure 6.5).

Figure 6.6: Postcard of the Maple Museum with the Maple Cabin to the rear at right ca. mid1960s (Author's Collection).

One word of mouth story has it that this sugarhouse was in fact once standing on Cary lands in North Danville and was dismantled piece by piece and rebuilt in front of the factory.[252] Located on the grounds between the Maple Cabin and Maple Grove Candies building and in front of the Cary Company plant on Portland Street, this sugarhouse housed a Maple Museum to attract, educate and entertain tourists.

Figure 6.7: Pamphlet promoting tours of the Maple Grove plant and Maple Museum, ca. 1960s (Author's Collection).

The museum ran a movie explaining how maple syrup was made and displayed tools used in the sugaring process.[253] Whaley's Maple Museum became a noteworthy attraction for St. Johnsbury and the Northeast Kingdom. Free guided tours of the plant and candy making operation proved to be very popular with summer tourists and travelers on Highway 2 (Figure 6.6). The Sugarhouse Maple Museum proved to be such a success at bringing in tourists that in 1956 alone, Maple Grove reported that it had hosted over 20,000 visitors.[254] Over sixty years later, the maple museum still stands as a centerpiece on the grounds of the Maple Grove Farms property (Figure 6.7).

Whaley came to the Cary Company during their bankruptcy, after having worked in advertising and promotions for a New York City candy company. At the Cary Company Whaley worked mostly on the Maple Grove Candies side of the company helping to come up with new ideas for sales and merchandise. One unique idea of Whaley's that became a signature product of Maple Grove was a small log cabin filled with maple sugar candies (Figure 6.8). This item was important enough to the company that Maple Grove and Whaley even went so far as to secure a patent on the container in 1934 (Figure 6.9). Described as a lively character, Whaley was an ardent supporter of Vermont products and companies. Although Whaley himself never claimed the title, one Vermont reporter once referred to Whaley as one of the "candy kings" of Vermont."[255]

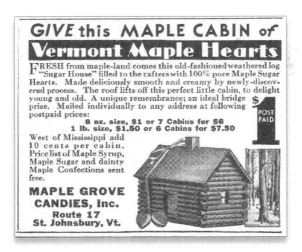

Figure 6.8: 1936 advertisement for Maple Grove Candies, Inc. (Author's Collection).

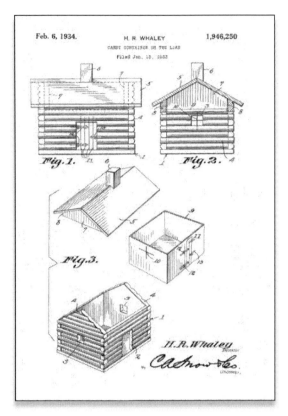

Figure 6.9: United States Patent No. 1,946,250 awarded to Harold R. Whaley for "Candy Container or the Like" (United States Patent Office website).

Cary Company Leaves but Maple Grove Stays

Edward Boylan continued in his new position as President of the Cary Company, and as planned, left St. Johnsbury, moved with the company to New York. However, after suffering through a few years of frustrating customer complaints and less attention to quality under Fred Fear and Company's ownership, Boylan had had enough and retired in 1957. Sadly, after over 30 years working with the Cary Company name, Boylan was not afforded a pension or severance pay of any kind.[256]

The sale and relocation of the Cary Company opened the door to a series of changes in ownership and marginalization of the Cary brand

and products. The year after Fred Fear & Company purchased the Cary Maple Sugar Company in 1953, Fred Fear & Company was sold to The Childs Company, the parent company for Childs Restaurants, an east coast restaurant chain that came to prominence in the 1920s and 1930s.[257] In 1966, Fred Fear & Company, as a subsidiary of The Childs Company, sold the Cary Maple Sugar Company and operations along with the Cary's brand to HCA Food Corporation, owner of the Doxsee Seafood Company. The HCA Food Corporation in turn quickly sold it to Specialty Brands of America, Inc. in the late 1960s.

Through the 1950s and into the 1960s under the ownership of Fred Fear & Company, Childs, and HCA Food Corporation, the Cary Maple Sugar Company continued as owners of the St. Johnsbury plant. The company primarily used the plant for receiving and storing of maple syrup, albeit in a very limited capacity compared to the volumes and activities of earlier years. In the 1950s the plant continued to handle around three to four million pounds of maple syrup a year purchased in the United States and Canada, with the bulk of their purchases coming from Canadian producers. The company was also using only a portion of the plant and was renting out unused space in the building for the storage of heavy electrical appliances.[258] At one point there was consideration of vacating the entire second floor, moving their equipment to the third floor and freeing up 10,000 square feet for a prospective tenant. By the later 1950s the crew working for the Cary Company plant had been reduced to five plant workers and two office workers.[259] In the 1970s and 1980s, Peck's Hardware operated out of a portion of the Cary Company Plant. Today it is not uncommon for long-time St. Johnsbury residents to refer to that portion of Cary plant as the Peck's Building or Peck's Hardware Building rather than the Cary Plant or Maple Grove.

Herbert Whaley continued to own and operate Maple Grove in St. Johnsbury for the remainder of his life. He died in 1972 and in 1975 the Whaley family sold Maple Grove to William F. Callahan, III who owned and operated the business until 1998. Under Callahan's ownership, the name was changed in 1985 from Maple Grove to Maple Grove Farms.[260] While still making maple candies and bottling maple syrup, Callahan was also instrumental in leading the company to expand their product lines to include a sugar-free syrup as well as other "lite" and fat-free salad dressings and a waffle mix.

Although Callahan was not afraid to expand the scope of Maple Grove to include more than maple products, at the same time he was sensitive to and interested in recognizing the historical significance of the Cary plant. In 1984 Callahan contacted the Division for Historic Preservation of the Vermont Historical Society, requesting a review of the National Register eligibility of the Maple Grove and Cary buildings comprising what was once the Cary Maple Sugar Company complex. The Division for Historic Preservation replied that it was their opinion that the building complex was eligible for nomination to the National Register of Historic Places and advised Callahan of the process of securing a formal evaluation and completion of the appropriate nomination forms and documentation by a qualified architectural historian.

Unfortunately, it does not appear that efforts were ever made to follow-up and complete the official evaluation and nomination. Although some interior and exterior changes have been made to the buildings comprising the Cary Maple Sugar Company complex, they are remarkably unchanged in comparison to their original 1920s forms.[261]

Had Callahan hired an architectural historian to document the complex they would probably have described the Cary plant as an example of the "Daylight Factory" style of industrial architecture, a common building style in the first thirty years of the twentieth century. Like most other daylight factory buildings, the Cary plant was also an example of a modern multi-floor, fire-proof structure built with steel reinforced concrete piers and concrete floors, with large banks of windows above a modest brick spandrel panel to allow in light and air. These factories feature open floor plans with rows of mushrooming concrete columns.[262] Over time the Cary plant has seen some modifications and removals to the defining elements of a daylight factory as well as other features unique to the location. The tall brick smokestack with the word "Cary" painted in bold black letters that once billowed black smoke from the ever-burning boilers was removed many years ago, and the simple, barn-like wood plank warehouses and outer buildings have been demolished or replaced with modern and more substantial structures. The brick two-story Maple Grove building looks remarkably the same both inside and out as it did when it was built in 1929. As with most continually occupied industrial facilities that evolves over time, the buildings of the complex do not appear exactly as they did when built. However, their primary look and features have been preserved, and the major buildings, including; the Cary plant, the Maple Grove building, the Maple Cabin, the Maple Guest House and the Maple Museum, are still intact. This warrants continued consideration for nomination to the National Register of Historic Properties.

Together Again
After over twenty years of ownership, Callahan sold Maple Grove Farms to the food conglomerate B & G Foods, Incorporated in 1998, reportedly for $20 million. B & G Foods' addition of Maple Grove Farms to their corporate family expanded their existing syrup product line which already included Vermont Maid and Brer Rabbit brand syrups. As more than simply a syrup and candy company, Maple Grove Farms continued and expanded their existing sales of pure maple syrup, maple candies, pancake and waffle mixes, and salad dressings, leading to revenues of $50 million in 2000 then increasing those to $65 million in 2002. By 2014, Maple Grove Farms' net sales had risen to $79 million with nearly all the production and packaging happening in the St. Johnsbury facilities.[263]

In the new century, the Cary's brand continued to be a subsidiary of Specialty Brands of America, but in one final shift in ownership for the Cary's label, Specialty Brands of America sold the Cary's Company to B & G Foods in early 2014. With B & G Foods adding the Cary's brand to its maple syrup product line, the Maple Grove and Cary's brands were back together again under one roof for the first time since they were split in 1953.

Over the years, Maple Grove Farms has expanded beyond just making and selling maple products; however, it is still a maple products company at heart. According to Mark Bigelow, Maple Grove Farms plant manager in St. Johnsbury, even today, the majority of Maple Grove's business is still maple products, with approximately 65 percent coming from maple syrup sales.[264]

7

Legacy of a Maple King

The story and legacy of George Cary's maple empire spanned five decades, beginning in the late 1800s, continuing through to the twenty-first century. Even with its share of bumps, delays, and distractions along the way, thanks to the ground work of George Cary, St. Johnsbury became and continues to be a central node in the larger network of maple production in North America.

As this book has shown, Cary led a transformation of the maple sugar and syrup industry in the late nineteenth and early twentieth centuries by introducing new markets and outlets for maple products at a time when the industry was going through a serious decline. As noted in David Leff's book *Maple Sugaring: Keeping It Real in New England*," in 1818, maple sugar was half the price of cane, and by 1880 they were equal. By 1885, cane was cheaper for the first time. Maple continued to be consumed on the farms and in rural regions, but price and easy availability, along with the notion that maple was outdated and old fashioned, made cane the undisputed choice in growing urban areas."[265] While it is gratuitous to attribute the survival of the modern maple syrup industry to one man, it is fair to argue that George Cary did more than any other individual at the time to advance and modernize an industry that was in decline.

The fortuitous transaction by Cary of trading an order of groceries for maple sugar that was in turn sold for curing of tobacco kept open the door for the maple producers to continue their time-honored springtime production. This development of a market of using maple sugar for curing tobacco served as a kind of bridging industry for maple producers while the industry realigned itself on the heels of being out priced by cane sugar, and transitioned maple syrup into a specialty condiment and gourmet food or flavoring ingredient.

Cary was able to establish a new maple sugar market quickly by engaging previously disconnected industries, employing methods and scales of production not previously considered, and backing it all with strong capitalization. In time, Cary brought a corporate business model to the industry, working with significantly larger national clients like the American Tobacco Company and Towle's Maple Products Company. He also added secondary maple related companies to the Cary Company portfolio, most notably Maple Grove Candies and the Brower Sap Pipeline System.

With small-scale maple sugar production transitioning to a maple syrup industry in the early twentieth century, many maple producers took a rather dim view to the also developing blended syrup industry. Adulteration and false claims of pure maple syrup by blended syrup makers were certainly unfair competition and cause for concern by the pure maple syrup makers. The use of maple sugar and syrup for legitimate blending of table syrups was considered by producers to be supporting the competition for the limited market share of syrup consumers, causing the pure maple syrup industry to be cheated. However, Cary knew that there were different preferences among consumers in the United States and Canada and this was just part of the business of selling as much maple syrup and maple sugar as possible.

Understanding this bigger picture, Cary held a seat on the Board of Directors for Towle's, the maker of Log Cabin Syrup. Working hand in hand with the Log Cabin company, Cary was instrumental in Towle's operating a bottling plant in St. Johnsbury for several years. George

Cary's relationship with the Towle Company continued even after the company left St. Johnsbury. George Cary's daughter, Madeline Cary recalled how W. J. Towle sent George Cary a plaque in 1921 in appreciation for his assistance in financially helping the floundering Towle Company in years past. According to Madeline[266], the plaque read:

> A Man Came Out of the East
> He went back heavily burdened, but smiling,
> Leaving Peace, Happiness and Tranquility

Following the exit of the Towle Maple Products Company from St. Johnsbury in the nineteen-teens, Cary began a push to move maple producers away from producing maple sugar in the sugarbushes and sugarhouses, and towards producing bulk maple syrup to be packed into metal barrels and bought and sold by the pound. While something of a secondary product in their business model at the time, the Cary Company also began to bottle and can Highland Syrup, its own brand of pure maple syrup.

In addition to the shift to maple syrup in barrels, Cary and packers like him were instrumental in pushing for and putting in place uniform grading requirements for labeling syrup. Having these grades in place helped bring about improved consistency and clarity to the process of buying syrup as well as assisted in easier blending.

The modern telling of the history of Maple Grove Farms emphasizes the roles of the three women that started it as a home candy company and largely ignores the contribution of George Cary. This is an interesting and more recent choice of historical narratives by the people at Maple Grove Farms and B & G Foods. For example, as recently as 1955, Maple Grove's past owner, Harold Whaley, continued to tell the story of Cary's initial tobacco for sugar deal as a part of the origins of the Maple Grove Company.[267] It is understandable how the community and future owners might be inclined to minimize the Cary origins to the history of Maple Grove. After all, the Cary Company departure was a blow to the community, whereas the Maple Grove Company stayed the course and stuck with the community. However, as was shown in earlier chapters, Cary was instrumental in the early growth of Maple Grove Candies and brought the company to the next level, both as an investor and then by purchasing the company outright and bringing it into the fold of the larger Cary Company. Ironically, it was the Maple Grove Company that continued to evolve into a more successful brand in the latter half of the 20th century, while over time the Cary Company and the Cary label declined in importance and market share in the maple syrup industry.

Cary as a man may have come across as gruff, uncompromising, and very self-assured, maybe to a fault, but he was also able to see a bigger picture for the industry beyond the limits of the sugarbush or the state. It would be easy to call him visionary, which is probably an overstatement, because he was more conservative in his approach to leading and reacting to change. It would be fair to call him a leader, both through his overwhelming control of the bulk maple products market, but more importantly as a man to whom people looked for answers, direction, and support for the current and future state of the industry. Unlike some of his more reserved New England neighbors, Cary was not reluctant to promote his name and his activities. One gets a sense that for Cary this was both a marketing strategy and marker of personal vanity.

Beyond the maple industry, the legacy of George Cary and his family continues in St. Johnsbury. In 1985, George Cary's daughter Madeline Cary Fleming made a generous gift to the St. Johnsbury Academy of over $250,000. All three of George and Annie Cary's children had attended the Academy at one time or another. In recognition of the gift, the Academy named one of their athletic facilities Cary Field. A small monument at the field contains a dedication that reads "Cary Field in memory of George Cary, who made St. Johnsbury the maple center of the country, and to his wife Annie, who did much for the educational, church, and social welfare of the community."

The story and legacy Cary persists in other forms around the village and county. In addition to the naming of Cary Field at St. Johnsbury Academy and of Cary Place, the short street adjacent to the Cary home on Main Street in St. Johnsbury, the Cary name can still be found on the landscape and maps of North Danville where Cary Brook and Cary Pond are located in the vicinity of what was once Cary's Highland Farm. In 1975 the Cary home on Main Street was listed on the National Register of Historic Places as a contributing structure to the St. Johnsbury Main Street Historic District and more recently has been going through a careful historically accurate restoration by its current owners.[268] Even though the Maple Grove name is now the name that is prominently displayed at the former Cary plant on the eastern edge of St. Johnsbury and the Cary name is no longer visible in big letters atop the roof or along the once prominent smokestack, George Cary and the importance of the company he built is lodged in the memories of most of the village's citizens.

Through his decision to locate in St. Johnsbury and his ongoing promotion of the Cary Maple Sugar Company as a Vermont company, Cary helped solidify the idea in the minds of Americans that Vermont is the homeland of maple syrup. After all, the Maple King and the Maple Capital were founded in Vermont. It seemed only fitting that Vermont must be the cultural and industrial center of the maple industry.

NOTES

Preface

[1] Matthew M. Thomas, with contributions, *An Archaeological Overview of Native American Maple Sugaring and Historic Sugarbushes of the Lac du Flambeau Band of Lake Superior Chippewa Indians*. Report submitted to the Division of Historic Preservation of the State Historical Society of Wisconsin in partial fulfillment of Survey and Planning Grant no. 55-98-13157-2. (Lac du Flambeau Tribal Historic Preservation Office and the George W. Brown, Jr. Ojibwe Museum and Cultural Center, 1999).

[2] Matthew M. Thomas, "The Archaeology of Great Lakes Native American Maple Sugar Production in the Reservation Era," *The Wisconsin Archeologist* 82 (2001): 75-102.

[3] Matthew M. Thomas, Kelly Anderson, and Marcus Guthrie, "Historic Native American Maple Sugaring Camps in the Western Great Lakes: An Integrated Approach to their Identification and Interpretation" (paper presented at the Society for American Archaeology Annual Meeting, Chicago, IL. April 1999).

[4] Thomas, Matthew, "The Gooseneck Metal Pipeline: Wisconsin's First Tubing System?" *Wisconsin Maple News* 20 (2004): 12.

[5] Matthew M, Thomas, "*Where the Forest Meets the Farm: A Comparison of the Spatial and Historical Change in the Euro-American and American Indian Maple Production Landscape*" (doctoral dissertation, University of Wisconsin-Madison, 2004).

[6] Matthew M. Thomas, "A History of the Gooseneck: The Brower Sap Piping System and the Cary Maple Syrup Company," *Maple Syrup Digest* October 17A (2005):25-30.

[7] Harry Richardson, unnamed film, 1927, *Philippe Beaudry Collection*, (Northeast Historic Film Bucksport, ME). Copies of the film are on file and can be viewed for non-commercial research and education purposes in the Vermont Historical Society archives, the St. Johnsbury Athenaeum, Bailey Howe Library Special Collections at the University of Vermont.

[8] Charlie Welcome, *Cary Maple Sugar Company, St. Johnsbury, Vermont*. Unpublished manuscript, n.d.

Chapter One: Introduction

[9] John A. Hitchcock, *Economics of the Farm Manufacture of Maple Syrup and Sugar*, Bulletin 285, Vermont Agricultural Experiment Station (1928).

[10] Ron Strickland, "Everett Palmer: Sugarmaker," *Vermonters: Oral Histories from Down Country to the Northeast Kingdom*. (Hanover, University Press of New England, 1986) 116.

[11] Michael Farrell, *The Future of the Maple Sugar Industry in the United States: Assessing the Growth Potential Based on Ecologic, Economic, Demographic, and Public Policy Factors*, Cornell University Department of Natural Resources, Uihlein Forest (n.d.), http://www.cornellmaple.com.

[12] The assignment of the title of Maple King to George C. Cary appeared as early as 1901. "Local Gatherings," *St. Johnsbury Caledonian* (St. Johnsbury, VT), October 1, 1901.

[13] In this book, the term maple sugaring is used as a catch all term for the process of manufacturing any maple sap related product, which may include various forms of maple sugar, maple syrup, maple cream, etc. Similarly, sugarmakers are the people engaged in the process of maple sugaring.

[14] William F. Fox and William F. Hubbard, *The Maple Sugar Industry*, U.S. Department of Agriculture Bureau of Forestry Bulletin 59 (1905).

[15] In 1906 the Pure Food and Drug Act made it illegal to label something pure maple syrup if it was a blend of maple and cane sugar.

[16] David W. Babson, "Sweet Spring: The Development and Meaning of Maple Syrup Production at Fort Drum, New York" (doctoral dissertation, Syracuse University 2010), 256-257.

[17] David W. Babson, "Sweet Spring: The Development and Meaning of Maple Syrup Production at Fort Drum, New York" (doctoral dissertation, Syracuse University 2010), 89.

[18] Michael Lange, "*Meanings of Maple: An Ethnography of Sugaring*," University of Arkansas Press (Fayetteville, AR) 2017.

[19] Mary R. P. Hatch, "St. Johnsbury, Vermont and Its Industries," *New England Magazine* 33 Sept 1905- Feb. 1906: 740; Hitchcock, *Economics of Farm Manufacture* 1928.

[20] Edward T. Fairbanks, *The Town of St. Johnsbury, VT: A Review of One Hundred Twenty-Five Years to the Anniversary Pageant 1912* (The Cowles Press, St. Johnsbury, 1929) 491.

[21] *Highland Maple Syrup Recipes from Old Vermont*, (Cary Maple Sugar Company. St. Johnsbury, VT 1939).

[22] For a clear and detailed presentation of the organization of the modern maple syrup industry see Douglass Whynott, *The Sugar Season: A Year in the Life of Maple Syrup, and One Family's Quest for the Sweetest Harvest*, Da Capo Press (Philadelphia, PA, 2014).

Chapter Two: Formation of the Kingdom

[23] Lois Greer, "America's Maple King: George C. Cary," *The Vermonter* 34, no. 1 (1929): 3-8; Edward Sherburne Doubleday, "Highlights in the History of the Cary Maple Sugar Company," *Maple Syrup Digest* 2a, no. 2 (1990): 18-21; James M. Lawrence and Rux Martin, *Sweet Maple: Life, lore & recipes from the sugarbush*, (Shelburne, VT, Chapters Publishing, 1993); Betty Ann Lockhart, *Maple Sugarin' In Vermont: A Sweet Story*, The History Press, 2008); Peggy Pearl, *A Brief History of St. Johnsbury*, (Charleston, SC, The History Press, 2009).

[24] *George C. Cary: President, Cary Maple Sugar Company, St. Johnsbury, Vermont*. Unreferenced, biography in George C. Cary Papers, Fairbanks Museum Archives (St. Johnsbury, VT 1925/1926).

[25] Lois Goodwin Greer, "America's Maple Sugar King: George C. Cary," *The Vermonter* Vol. 34, No. 1: 3-8 (1929).

[26] "News About Home," *St. Johnsbury Caledonian* (St. Johnsbury, VT), February 15, 1895.

[27] It is not clear what the cause of death was for young Teresa Cary; Madeline Aldrich Cary, *Biographical Sketch of George and Annie* Cary. George C. Cary Papers, Fairbanks Museum Archives (St. Johnsbury, VT 1976).

[28] "State News," Middlebury Register (Middlebury, VT), December 18, 1896;

[29] *Claire Dunne Johnson papers* – 6/6/83, Fairbanks Museum Archives (St. Johnsbury, VT).

[30] "Local Gatherings," *St. Johnsbury Caledonian* (St. Johnsbury, VT), October 29, 1897; "Local Gatherings," *St. Johnsbury Caledonian* (St. Johnsbury, VT), July 13, 1898.

[31] "George C. Cary," *St. Johnsbury Caledonian* (St. Johnsbury, VT), November 7, 1900.

[32] "Local News – Morrisville," *News and Citizen* (Morrisville, VT), April 10, 1901.

[33] "Local Gatherings," *St. Johnsbury Caledonian* (St. Johnsbury, VT), July 23, 1902.

[34] Maple Sugar and Syrup Buyers Contract between T.W. Hale and Cary Company, January 27, 1907. From the personal collections of the author.

[35] "Cary Maple Sugar Co.," *St. Johnsbury Directory* (St. Johnsbury, VT), 1901.

[36] In its early years Log Cabin syrup contained 45 percent maple syrup but by 1950 that percentage had been reduced to about 15 percent, and today the Log Cabin Company will confirm that their syrup does contain some maple syrup, but they refuse to disclose in what percentage. James Trager, *The Food Chronology: A Food Lover's Compendium of Events and Anecdotes, from Prehistory to Present* (New York, Henry Holt and Company, 1995) 326; Hovey Burgess, "The Blended Maple Sirup Industry", *Report of Proceedings of the Conference on Maple Products* (Philadelphia, PA, 1950).

[37] "George C. Cary," *St. Johnsbury Caledonian* (St. Johnsbury, VT), November 7, 1900.

[38] "Local Gatherings," *St. Johnsbury Caledonian* (St. Johnsbury, VT), October 1, 1901.

[39] "Maple Sugar Company with $125,000 Capital," *Vermont Phoenix* (Brattleboro, VT), December 16, 1904.

[40] Ezra S. Stearns, *Genealogical and Family History of the State of New Hampshire*, Vol. III (New York: Lewis Publishing Co., 1908) 1115-1116; "New Hampshire Necrology – Fred P. Virgin," *The Granite Monthly* 40, No. 7: 259; "Personals," *St. Johnsbury Caledonian* (St. Johnsbury, VT), March 3, 1909.

[41] "Cary," *New England Families and Genealogical Memorials*, Vol. III., William Richard Cutter, Compiler, (Lewis Historical Publishing Company: New York, 1914), 1526.

[42] Cary," *New England Families and Genealogical Memorials*, Vol. III., William Richard Cutter, Compiler, (Lewis Historical Publishing Company: New York, 1914), 1526; Prentiss Cutler Dodge, "George C. Cary," *Encyclopedia of Vermont Biography: A Series of Authentic Biographical Sketches of the Representative Men of Vermont and Sons of Vermont in Other States* (Burlington, VT: Ullery Publishing Company 1912), 141; "St. Johnsbury Caucuses," *St. Johnsbury Caledonian* (St. Johnsbury, VT) June 13, 1906; "The Telephone Situation," *St. Johnsbury Caledonian* (St. Johnsbury, VT) October 21, 1908.

[43] Newcomb, Fish and Cary Make Stirring Addresses at Armory," *St. Johnsbury Caledonian* (St. Johnsbury, VT) June 27, 1917.

[44] Madeline Aldrich Cary, *Biographical Sketch of George and Annie* Cary. George C. Cary Papers, Fairbanks Museum Archives (St. Johnsbury, VT 1976).

[45] "St. Johnsbury's Fat Men's Club," *St. Johnsbury Caledonian* (St. Johnsbury, VT), July 6, 1910; Madeline Aldrich Cary, *Biographical Sketch of George and Annie* Cary. George C. Cary Papers, Fairbanks Museum Archives (St. Johnsbury, VT 1976).

[46] King of Maple Sugar, Hustler: George C. Cary, One-Time Drummer, Now Rich Man, Works From 8 A.M. to Midnight, *The Boston Post*, (Boston, MA), March 22, 1926.

[47] Madeline Aldrich Cary, *Biographical Sketch of George and Annie* Cary. George C. Cary Papers, Fairbanks Museum Archives (St. Johnsbury, VT 1976).

[48] ; Madeline Aldrich Cary, *Biographical Sketch of George and Annie* Cary. George C. Cary Papers, Fairbanks Museum Archives (St. Johnsbury, VT 1976).

[49] Arthur F. Stone, "Clinton P. Cary," *The Vermont of Today: With Its Historical Background, Attractions, and People – Vol. III* (Lewis Historical Publishing Co. Inc., New York: 1929); St. Luke's School closed in 1927; Madeline Cary Fleming, *Biographical Sketch of Clinton Partridge Cary*. George C. Cary Papers, Fairbanks Museum Archives (St. Johnsbury, VT 1976).

[50] Madeline Cary Fleming, *Biographical Sketch of Clinton Partridge Cary*. George C. Cary Papers, Fairbanks Museum Archives (St. Johnsbury, VT 1976).

[51] Madeline Cary Fleming, *Biographical Sketch of Clinton Partridge Cary*. George C. Cary Papers, Fairbanks Museum Archives (St. Johnsbury, VT 1976); "Young Milk Merchants," *St. Johnsbury Caledonian* (St. Johnsbury, VT) July 17, 1907; Vermont's Famous Steers," *St. Johnsbury Caledonian* (St. Johnsbury, VT) September 29, 1909.

[52] Nancy Cary Aldrich interview, January 29, 2015.

[53] "Local Gatherings," *St. Johnsbury Caledonian* (St. Johnsbury, VT), February 6, 1901; Property Transaction notes - Claire Dunne Johnson papers, Fairbanks Museum Archives (St. Johnsbury, VT).

[54] "Business Notes," *St. Johnsbury Caledonian* (St. Johnsbury, VT), October 4, 1899; "Personals," *St. Johnsbury Caledonian* (St. Johnsbury, VT), October 11, 1899.

[55] "The Building Outlook," *St. Johnsbury Caledonian* (St. Johnsbury, VT), April 17, 1901.

[56] "The Farmer's Line" *St. Johnsbury Caledonian* (ST. Johnsbury, VT), November 20, 1901.

[57] "29 Cattle Killed," *Spirit of the Age* (Woodstock, VT), July 6, 1901; "Fire at Lookout Farm," *St. Johnsbury Caledonian* (St. Johnsbury, VT), July 3, 1901; "Local Gatherings," *St. Johnsbury Caledonian* (St. Johnsbury, VT), July 10, 1901.

[58] "Mr. Cary's New Herd," *St. Johnsbury Caledonian* (St. Johnsbury, VT), July 23, 1902.

[59] "Auction Sale," *St. Johnsbury Caledonian* (St. Johnsbury, VT), September 16, 1903.

60 Four Corners is the area around the intersection of Gos Hollow Road and Mt. Pleasant Street or Crepeault Road. Now lost to a fire, the Four Corners School once stood near this intersection. "Real Estate Transactions," *St. Johnsbury Caledonian* (St. Johnsbury, VT), June 3, 1903; "Local Gatherings," *St. Johnsbury Caledonian* (St. Johnsbury, VT), July 15, 1903; Madeline Aldrich Cary, *Biographical Sketch of George and Annie* Cary. George C. Cary Papers, Fairbanks Museum Archives (St. Johnsbury, VT 1976).

61 Madeline Aldrich Cary, *Biographical Sketch of George and Annie* Cary. George C. Cary Papers, Fairbanks Museum Archives (St. Johnsbury, VT 1976).

62 "Local Gatherings," *St. Johnsbury Caledonian* (St. Johnsbury, VT), August 2, 1899.

63 "Business Notes," *St. Johnsbury Caledonian* (St. Johnsbury, VT), September 5, 1900.

64 It is possible that this report is mistaken in stating that the Lookout Farm was adjacent to the Drew farm when in fact it was Cary's Highland or Batchelder Farm that was located adjacent. It is true that the Lookout Farm was in the same area of North Danville and may also have been adjacent in some form to the Drew Farm. "Local Gatherings," *St. Johnsbury Caledonian* (St. Johnsbury, VT), November 27, 1901.

65 F.W. Beers, *County Atlas of Caledonia, Vermont – from actual surveys by and under the direction of F.W. Beers*. (New York) 1875.

66 "Local Gatherings," *St. Johnsbury Caledonian* (St. Johnsbury, VT) November 25, 1914.

67 F.W. Beers, *County Atlas of Caledonia, Vermont – from actual surveys by and under the direction of F.W. Beers*. (New York) 1875.

68 "North Danville – Old Grist Mill Being Torn Down," *St. Johnsbury Caledonian* (St. Johnsbury, VT) November 19, 1913.

69 National Register of Historic Places Inventory – Nomination Form – Broadview Farm, Caledonia County, VT. NRHP Reference No. 83004224 Nominated October 25, 1983

70 "Record-Breaking Show Now On," *Evening Caledonian* (St. Johnsbury, VT), September 23, 1919.

71 "Horse Gossip," *St. Johnsbury Caledonian* (St. Johnsbury, VT), July 6, 1898; Madeline Aldrich Cary, *Biographical Sketch of George and Annie* Cary. George C. Cary Papers, Fairbanks Museum Archives (St. Johnsbury, VT 1976).

72 "Another Herd in New England. – George C. Cary Starts With Herefords at St. Johnsbury, VT.," *The American Hereford Journal*, Vol. 10, No. 5 (1919).

73 "Stock For Chicago Exhibit," St. Johnsbury Caledonian (St. Johnsbury, VT) November 11, 1911; "Won Prizes at Chicago," *St. Johnsbury Caledonian* (St. Johnsbury, VT) December 20, 1911;

74 "Record-Breaking Crowd Attends Greatest Fair in County's History," *Evening Caledonian* (St. Johnsbury, VT), September 24, 1919.

75 "Local Gatherings," *St. Johnsbury Caledonian* (St. Johnsbury, VT) September 30, 1914.

76 Letter from Stephen Jones to Matthew Thomas 2005. Stephen Jones, the current owner of the former Stanton sugarbush on Cary's Highland Farm recalled that when hiking through many miles of the woods of the area of the Highland Farm in 1979 and 1980 he encountered the remnants of a variety of sugarhouses and piles of metal tubing from the Brower pipeline system. Jones also spoke with many of the older residents and landowners at the time who reported on the past locations of a number of Cary sugarhouses and workers camps in the woods around Highland Farm.

77 In the late 1930s, the three Zabarsky brothers from the very successful St. Johnsbury Trucking Company family bought the property and later developed Woodland Lodge as an extensive modern summer residence and retreat for their families complete with several cabins, outbuildings, and an in-ground Olympic size swimming pool. The Zabarsky family donated their 102.7 acre Woodland Lodge estate to the St. Johnsbury Academy, who presently own and operate the Lodge. Over the years the Academy's use of the property has adjusted to meet their needs and the needs of their students, both providing programs for special needs students and a scholars program for advanced academics. The sugarbush surrounding Woodland Lodge continues to be tapped since the 1990s by the Goodrich Maple Farm which tap as many as 6000 trees on the property. Maurice Zabarsky Interview January 13, 2005. The St. Johnsbury Academy's ownership of Woodland Lodge has not been continuous. The 102.7 acre property was initially donated to the Academy in 1971 by the Zabarsky family, but due to unmanageable operating costs, the Academy sold the property in 1981. A single family owned and resided at the property from 1981 to 1993 when they repurchased it from the family and re-incorporated its facilities in their activities and teaching programs. Personal Communication with William Cruess, Assistant headmaster St. Johnsbury Academy, January 12, 2005.

Chapter Three: Expansion of the Kingdom

78 "A Growing Business," *St. Johnsbury Caledonian* (St. Johnsbury, VT) May 3, 1905; Cary Maple Sugar Company letterhead dated June 14, 1907, from the personal collections of the author.

79 "Short Locals," *Commercial Advertiser* (Canton, NY), March 3, 1908.

80 "Queen of the White River Valley, Rochester, A Town of Opportunity," *The Vermonter*, Vol. 15, No. 1 (1910): 7-21.

81 *The Cary Maple Sugar Company, Appelle, v. The Pierre Viau Maple Company, Appellant*, 173 Ill. App. S4, (October 1912).

82 Mary R.P. Hatch, "St. Johnsbury, Vermont and Its Industries," *New England Magazine* vol. 33, Sept 1905 to Feb. 1906: 734-750.

83 "Sugar Maker," *St. Johnsbury Caledonian* (St. Johnsbury, VT), March 27, 1912.

84 "The Maple Sugar Situation," *St. Johnsbury Caledonian* (St. Johnsbury, VT), April 17, 1901. Sherb Doubleday described similar unscrupulous methods used by sugarmakers in the past to increase the weight of their bulk sugar sales to dealers, Sherb Doubleday, "Reflections," *Maple Syrup Digest* 6A, no. 1 (1994): 20-24.

85 Clinton P. Cary, *C.P.C.'s Talk at Rotary Luncheon, October 15, 1929*, Manuscript found in George C. Cary Papers, Fairbanks Museum Archives (St. Johnsbury, VT).

86 Letter from Cary Maple Sugar Company to Sugar Buyers, December 1, 1919. From the private collections of Tom Olson, Rutland, VT.

87 Letter from Cary Maple Sugar Company to Sugar Buyers, November 14, 1921. From the private collections of Tom Olson, Rutland, VT.

88 Clinton P. Cary, *C.P.C.'s Talk at Rotary Luncheon, October 15, 1929*, Manuscript found in George C. Cary Papers, Fairbanks Museum Archives (St. Johnsbury, VT).

89 Sherb Doubleday, "Reflections," *Maple Syrup Digest* vol. 6A, No. 1, 1994.

[90] "Lots of Maple Sugar – Extensive Industry in Northern Somerset Not Generally Known," *The Somerset Reporter* (Skowhegan, ME) 1908; Clinton P. Cary, *C.P.C.'s Talk at Rotary Luncheon, October 15, 1929*, Manuscript found in George C. Cary Papers, Fairbanks Museum Archives (St. Johnsbury, VT).

[91] Clinton P. Cary, *C.P.C.'s Talk at Rotary Luncheon, October 15, 1929*, Manuscript found in George C. Cary Papers, Fairbanks Museum Archives (St. Johnsbury, VT).

[92] Clinton P. Cary, *C.P.C.'s Talk at Rotary Luncheon, October 15, 1929*, Manuscript found in George C. Cary Papers, Fairbanks Museum Archives (St. Johnsbury, VT).

[93] *Maple Products: Investigation into an Alleged Combine in the Purchase of Maple Syrup and maple Sugar in the Province of Quebec*, Report of Commissioner, Combines Investigation Act, Department of Justice, Ottawa (1953).

[94] "Old-Fashioned Swap Started Cary on Way to be "Maple Sugar King,"" *Boston Sunday Globe* (Boston, MA) October 20, 1929.

[95] "Packing Maple Sugar," *Essex County Herald* (Guildhall, VT), April 5, 1918.

[96] "Local Gatherings," *St. Johnsbury Caledonian* (St. Johnsbury, VT), February 2, 1910; "Business Activity – Towle Maple Products Company Working Overtime," *St. Johnsbury Caledonian* (St. Johnsbury, VT) November 8, 1911.

[97] "Will Enlarge Plant. – Head of Towle Maple Products Company Came Here to Inspect Property. – Will Erect New Building," *St. Johnsbury Caledonian* (St. Johnsbury, VT), March 16, 1910.

[98] "Business Activity – Towle Maple Products Company Working Overtime," *St. Johnsbury Caledonian* (St. Johnsbury, VT) November 8, 1911.

[99] "Greater Vermont Notes," *Burlington Free Press and Times* (Burlington, VT), April 17, 1913; "Towle Maple Products Company Has Leased Pillsbury Baldwin Plant," *St. Johnsbury Caledonian* (St. Johnsbury, VT), March 13, 1913; "Greater Vermont Notes," *The Burlington Free Press and Times* (Burlington, VT) April 17, 1913; "St. Johnsbury Vermont" *Western New England Magazine*, June No. 6 (1913): 272; Clair Dunne Johnson, *"I See By the Paper..." An Informal History of St. Johnsbury, VT*, (Cowles Press, St. Johnsbury, VT 1987) 224.

[100] Edward T. Fairbanks, "Business Notes – Maple Sugar," *The Town of St. Johnsbury, VT; A Review of One Hundred Twenty-Five Years to the Anniversary Pageant 1912* (St. Johnsbury, VT.: The Cowles Press 1929).

[101] "To Leave St. Johnsbury – Towle Maple Products Company to Open Factory in Chicago," *St. Johnsbury Caledonian* (St. Johnsbury, VT), December 30, 1914; "News of the State," *Essex County Herald* (Guildhall, VT), February 12, 1915.

[102] "George Cary's Enlarged Block,", *St. Johnsbury Caledonian* (St. Johnsbury, VT) November 28, 1917; "Contracts Awarded – Hartford, Vt.," *The American Contractor*, Vol. 38, No. 41: 44 (October 13, 1917).

[103] The farm of Katherine Ide Gray and her husband George M. Gray was commonly referred to as "The Wayside" and was located three miles south of St. Johnsbury on the road to Passumpsic in Waterford Township. This road was also referred to as Edge Hill Rd.

[104] Lois Goodwin Greer, "Katherine Ide Gray," *The Vermonter*, vol. 32, No. 11 (1927).

[105] "Vermont News," *Essex County Herald* (Guildhall, VT), December 10, 1915.

106 "Fresh Cream, Maple Sugar, and Butternuts," *St. Johnsbury Caledonian* (St. Johnsbury, VT) September 22, 1915; "A Way for the Children to Earn Money," *St. Johnsbury Caledonian* (St. Johnsbury, VT) October 20, 1915.

107 Edward Sherburne Doubleday, "Highlights in the History of the Cary Maple Sugar Co.", *Maple Syrup Digest* vol. 2A, No. 2 (1990).

108 "Big Candy Firm is Organized," *Evening Caledonian* (St. Johnsbury, VT), January 6, 1920; "Maple Grove Candies Co. Form Organization," *Evening Caledonian* (St. Johnsbury, VT) January 14, 1920.

109 "Big Candy Firm is Organized," *Evening Caledonian* (St. Johnsbury, VT), January 6, 1920; "St. Johnsbury Local News," *The Evening Caledonian-Record* (St. Johnsbury, VT), April 17, 1920.

110 "Big Candy Firm is Organized," *Evening Caledonian* (St. Johnsbury, VT), January 6, 1920; "Maple Grove Candies," *Confectioners Gazette*, Vol. 41, No. 457: 16 (1919); Peggy Pearl, *A Brief History of St. Johnsbury* (Charleston, SC,: The History Press 2009).

111 "Pinehurst Sold to Maple Grove Candy Company," *St. Johnsbury Caledonian* (St. Johnsbury, VT) June 2, 1920; Property Transaction notes - Claire Dunne Johnson papers, Fairbanks Museum Archives (St. Johnsbury, VT).

112 "Maple Grove Candies Opening," *Caledonian Record* (St. Johnsbury, VT) December 8, 1920.

113 "Maple Grove Candies Plant Have Opening," *Caledonian Record* (St. Johnsbury, VT) December 10, 1920.

114 "10,000 Maple Grove Visitors During Year," *Caledonian Record* (St. Johnsbury, VT) December 8, 1922.

115 "Maple Grove Restaurant Advertisement," *The New Yorker* (New York, NY) May 19, 1928; "Maple Grove Restaurant," *Daily Star* (Brooklyn, NY) March 21, 1931.

116 Maple Grove Restaurant menu card. On file in the Maple Grove collections, Fairbanks Museum Archives (St. Johnsbury, VT).

117 Patent Number 1,946,250 "Candy Container or the Like" United States Patent Office, Application January 13, 1933, Patent Date February 4, 1934.

118 "Sugar Factory and Possibility of Normal School," Weekly Caledonian (St. Johnsbury, VT) September 10, 1919.

119 "Cary Offers New Factory to Employ 100 Men," *Evening Caledonian* (St. Johnsbury, VT) September 5, 1919.

120 "Cary Offers New Factory to Employ 100 Men," *Evening Caledonian* (St. Johnsbury, VT) September 5, 1919.

121 "PRESS COMMENT," Evening Caledonian (St. Johnsbury, VT) September 13, 1919; "Make It Unanimous," Evening Caledonian (St. Johnsbury, VT) September 18, 1919; "Plant Exempted," *Evening Caledonian* (St. Johnsbury, VT) September 22, 1919.

122 "Working on New Cary Plant in Summerville," *St. Johnsbury Caledonian* (St. Johnsbury, VT) December 10, 1919.

123 "St. Johnsbury Locals," Caledonian Record (St. Johnsbury, VT) December 11, 1919; Charlie Welcome, *Cary Maple Sugar Company, St. Johnsbury, Vermont*. Unpublished manuscript, n.d.

124 "To the People of St. Johnsbury," *Caledonian Record* (St. Johnsbury, VT) May 6, 1920.

125 "Contracts Awarded," *The American Contractor: Business Journal of Construction*, vol. 41, Nos. 29 and 35.

126 "New Plant of Cary Maple Sugar Company," *Evening Caledonian* (St. Johnsbury, VT) April 7, 1920.
127 "New Plant of Cary Maple Sugar Company," *Evening Caledonian* (St. Johnsbury, VT) April 7, 1920.
128 "St. Johnsbury Local News," *Evening Caledonian-Record* (St. Johnsbury, VT) March 15, 1921.
129 "St. Johnsbury Local News," *Caledonian Record* (St. Johnsbury, VT) August 5, 1922.
130 Clinton P. Cary, *C.P.C.'s Talk at Rotary Luncheon, October 15, 1929*, Manuscript found in George C. Cary Papers, Fairbanks Museum Archives (St. Johnsbury, VT).
131 "Maple Inn Now Ready for Visitors," Caledonian Record (St. Johnsbury, VT) August 24, 1920. Cary was reported to own another log cabin tea room along the Mohawk Trail in Lennox, Massachusetts. Cary sold this business in 1922.
132 *Maple Cabin and Maple Cabin Inn Brochure*, George C. Cary Papers, Fairbanks Museum Archives (St. Johnsbury, VT).
133 *Maple Cabin and Maple Cabin Inn Brochure*, George C. Cary Papers, Fairbanks Museum Archives (St. Johnsbury, VT).
134 "Cary Resigns as Maple Sugar Co. Head," *The Burlington Free* Press (Burlington, VT) August 1, 1931.
135 V-04 H. R. Derick collection, "Southern Canada Power correspondence concerning the industrial development of Lennoxville, 1921- 1955", Lennoxville-Ascot Historical & Museum Society Archives.
136 V-04 H. R. Derick collection, "Southern Canada Power correspondence concerning the industrial development of Lennoxville, 1921- 1955", Lennoxville-Ascot Historical & Museum Society Archives.
137 Clinton P. Cary, *C.P.C.'s Talk at Rotary Luncheon, October 15, 1929*, Manuscript found in George C. Cary Papers, Fairbanks Museum Archives (St. Johnsbury, VT).
138 Kathleen Atto and Committee, compilers, *Lennoxville, Volume 1* (Lennoxville, Quebec: Lennoxville-Ascot Historical & Museum Society) 1975; "Purchase Factory: Asbestos Corporation Locates in Lennoxville," *The Montreal Gazette* (Montreal, Quebec) November 26, 1934.

Chapter Four: Growing the King's Army
139 George H. Clark, "Collect maple Sap By gravity", *New England Homestead*, January 1, 1921.
140 Matthew M. Thomas, "A History of the Gooseneck: The Brower Sap Piping System and the Cary Maple Sugar Company", *Maple Syrup Digest* vol. 71A, no. 3: 25-30. October 2005.
141 "Pipeline Used to Collect Sap," *Boston Sunday Post* (Boston, MA) March 28, 1920.
142 Pipeline Used to Collect Sap," *Boston Sunday Post* (Boston, MA) March 28, 1920.
143 *The Brower Sap Piping System, Manufactured by The Brower System Branch of the Cary Maple Sugar Company, St. Johnsbury, VT*. Booklet in private collection, copy in collections of the author.
144 "Wide-Awake Grange Wins First Prize," *Caledonian Record* (St. Johnsbury, VT) September 18, 1920.

145 Matthew Thomas, "The Gooseneck Metal Pipeline: Wisconsin's First Tubing System?" *Wisconsin Maple News* vol. 20, no 1: 12. (2004).

146 Matthew M. Thomas, "A History of the Gooseneck: The Brower Sap Piping System and the Cary Maple Sugar Company", *Maple Syrup Digest* vol. 71A, no. 3: 25-30. October 2005. Text on a museum display of the piping system at the New England Maple Museum suggests that the manufacture of the system discontinued in 1926 but there is no associated citation to verify this statement.

147 The Cary silent film was donated as 2,600 feet on four reels to Northeast Historic Film in 1997 by Philippe Beaudry of Longueuil, Quebec for safe and secure archiving. The reels included footage of the Vermont flood of 1927 and is archived under the title "Cary Maple Sugar Company –outtakes" in the Philippe Beaudry Collection at Northeast Historic Film. The film has been converted to VHS and DVD masters for safe handling and reproduction. Unfortunately, restrictions on reproducing still images from the film coupled with the poor quality of the images on the deteriorating film prevent the display many of the various scenes from the film, in particular, scenes from the interior of the Cary plant and activity at the Stanton and Waterman sugarhouses (see Chapter Five). However, many of the still photographs made by the Richardson's at the time of filming the moving picture display the same scenes in better quality. Copies of the film in DVD format are maintained at the Vermont Historical Society, UVM Bailey Howe Library, the Fairbanks Museum and Planetarium Archives and the St. Johnsbury Athenaeum for educational purposes.

148 Florence A. Kendall, "Moving Pictures of Maple Sugar Making," *The Vermonter*, Vol. 31, No. 9 (1926).

149 Lois Goodwin Greer, "America's Maple Sugar King: George C. Cary," *The Vermonter* Vol. 34, No. 1: 3-8 (1929); "Real Romance in VT. Maple Sugar Making: Three Epochs in Its Development Shown in Cary Camps" Unknown Newspaper, April 7, 1927. News clipping found in photocopy version of Cary Family Album in the George C. Cary Papers, Fairbanks Museum Archives (St. Johnsbury, VT).

150 "Real Romance in VT. Maple Sugar Making: Three Epochs in Its Development Shown in Cary Camps" Unknown Newspaper, April 7, 1927. News clipping found in photocopy version of Cary Family Album in the George C. Cary Papers, Fairbanks Museum Archives (St. Johnsbury, VT).

151 Cary obit story

152 Arthur F. Stone, "Vermont on Wheels," *The Vermont of Today: With Its Historical Background, Attractions, and People – Vol. VI* (Lewis Historical Publishing Co. Inc., New York: 1929).

153 Clare Dunne Johnson, *"I See by the Paper…": An Informal History of St. Johnsbury*, Vol. II (St. Johnsbury, The Cowles Press 1989) 68.

154 Madeline Cary Fleming, *Biographical Sketch of George and Annie Cary*. George C. Cary Papers, Fairbanks Museum Archives (St. Johnsbury, VT 1976).

155 "Vermont Maple Sugar Train Returns to Burlington," *The Lewiston Daily Sun* (Lewiston, Maine) May 29, 1926.

156 Harriet F. Fisher, "The Sugar Train Rolled across America Spreading the Word that Vermont Had Recovered from the Great Flood", *The North Star Monthly* vol. 16, No. 11: 26-27 (April 2005); Betty Ann Lockhart, Maple Sugarin' In Vermont: A Sweet History (Charleston, SC, The History Press) 154-156.

157 Harriet F. Fisher, "The Sugar Train Rolled across America Spreading the Word that Vermont Had Recovered from the Great Flood", *The North Star Monthly* vol. 16, No. 11: 26-27 (April 2005).

158 John A. Hitchcock, *Economics of the Farm manufacture of Maple Syrup and Sugar*, Bulletin 286, Vermont Agricultural Experiment Station, (1928).

159 John A. Hitchcock, *Cost and Profit in the Sugar Orchard*, Bulletin 292, Vermont Agricultural Experiment Station, (1929).

160 "New Cary Plant," Evening Caledonian (St. Johnsbury, VT), June 22, 1919.

161 "Vermont Maple Syrup Co. of St. Johnsbury," Caledonian Record (St. Johnsbury, VT) June 2, 1922.

162 "Maple Sugar Plant Sold," *The Journal and Republican* (Lowville, NY) January 24, 1929.

163 "St. Johnsbury Local News," *Caledonian Record* (St. Johnsbury, VT) March 12, 1922.

164 "Annual Meeting Cary Maple Sugar Co.," *Caledonian Record* (St. Johnsbury, VT) April 5, 1922.

165 "Local News," *Caledonian Record* (St. Johnsbury, VT) November 18, 1922.

166 Madeline Cary Fleming, *Biographical Sketch of Clinton Partridge Cary*. George C. Cary Papers, Fairbanks Museum Archives (St. Johnsbury, VT 1976).

167 "Maple Grove Co. Has $100,000 Capital," *The Burlington Free Press* (Burlington, VT) April 19, 1929.

168 "In the Business Department," *St. Johnsbury Caledonian* (St. Johnsbury, VT) April 13, 1910.

169 Clare Dunne Johnson, *"I See by the Paper…": An Informal History of St. Johnsbury*, Vol. II (St. Johnsbury, The Cowles Press 1989) 17.

170 Clare Dunne Johnson, *"I See by the Paper…": An Informal History of St. Johnsbury*, Vol. II (St. Johnsbury, The Cowles Press 1989) 79, 206.

171 Arthur F. Stone, "Harold E. Franklin," *The Vermont of Today: With Its Historical Background, Attractions, and People – Vol. III* (Lewis Historical Publishing Co. Inc., New York: 1929).

172 Clare Dunne Johnson, *"I See by the Paper…": An Informal History of St. Johnsbury*, Vol. II (St. Johnsbury, The Cowles Press 1989) 100

173 "Exempt New Candy Factory From Taxes," *The Burlington Free Press* (Burlington, VT) April 16, 1929.

174 Charlie Welcome, *Cary Maple Sugar Company, St. Johnsbury, Vermont*. Unpublished manuscript, n.d.

175 John A. Hitchcock, *Economics of the Farm manufacture of Maple Syrup and Sugar*, Bulletin 285, Vermont Agricultural Experiment Station, (1928).

Chapter Five: The King is Dead

176 Clinton P. Cary, *C.P.C.'s Talk at Rotary Luncheon, October 15, 1929*, Manuscript found in George C. Cary Papers, Fairbanks Museum Archives (St. Johnsbury, VT).

[177] Lowell Smith, *St. Johnsbury's Past and Present, Sesqui-Centennial Program and Pageant Synopsis,* St. Johnsbury, VT – One Hundred Fifty Years of Progress (St. Johnsbury, VT: The Cowels Press 1937).

[178] Lowell Smith, *St. Johnsbury's Past and Present, Sesqui-Centennial Program and Pageant Synopsis,* St. Johnsbury, VT – One Hundred Fifty Years of Progress (St. Johnsbury, VT: The Cowels Press 1937).

[179] Merrill, Charles A., "Old-Fashioned Swap Started Cary On Way to Be 'Maple Sugar King' ", *The Boston Sunday Globe* (Boston, MA) October 20, 1929.

[180] "Meeting of the Maple Syrup Division of the Syrup and Molasses Section, Tuesday Morning, January 17th, 1922," *The Canner* (Fifteenth Annual Meeting of the National Canners Association and Allied Industries) January 16 and 17, 1922.

[181] A.W. McKay, *Marketing Vermont Maple-Sap Products,* Bulleting 227, Vermont Agricultural Experiment Station (1922).

[182] John P. David, "Vermont's Maple Sugar Industry", *The Vermont Review* Vol. 1, No. 6: 139-141 (1927).

[183] Amos J. Eaton, "Report of Manager of Vermont Maple Products Co-Operative Exchange", *Report of the Proceedings of the Thirty-First Annual Meeting of the Vermont Maple Sugar Makers' Association* (Burlington, VT) 1924.

[184] "Tuesday Evening Session", *Report of the Proceedings of the Thirty-Fourth Annual Meeting of the Vermont Maple Sugar Makers' Association* (Burlington, VT) 1926, p. 8.

[185] "H.C. Comings Speaks", *Report of the Proceedings of the Thirty-Fourth Annual Meeting of the Vermont Maple Sugar Makers' Association* (Burlington, VT) 1926.

[186] "Vermont's Maple Interests," *The Burlington Free Press* (Burlington, VT) February 2, 1927; "Our Vermont Maple and Co-Operative Marketing," *The Burlington Free Press* (Burlington, VT) February 3, 1927; "How Producers of Vermont Maple Syrup and Sugar May Profit," *The Burlington Free Press* (Burlington, VT) February 16,1927.

[187] John A. Hitchcock, *Economics of the Farm manufacture of Maple Syrup and Sugar,* Bulletin 285, Vermont Agricultural Experiment Station, (1928).

[188] John P. David, "Vermont's Maple Sugar Industry", *The Vermont Review* Vol. 1, No. 6: 139-141 (1927).

[189] Jacques LaMarche, *Cyrille Vaillancourt: Homme d'action, Homme d'unité, Coopérérateur émérite (1892-1969),* La Fédération du Québec des Caisses Populaires Desjardins. 1979, p. 61-63.

[190] Jacques LaMarche, *Cyrille Vaillancourt: Homme d'action, Homme d'unité, Coopérérateur émérite (1892-1969),* La Fédération du Québec des Caisses Populaires Desjardins. 1979, p. 61-63.

[191] "Government of Canada commemorates the annual production of maple products as an event of national historic significance" and "Maple Products," New Releases and Backgrounders, Parks Canada, October 17, 2009, modified September 26, 2013: http://www.pc.gc.ca/APPS/CP-NR/release_e.asp?bgid=1237&andor1=bg ; "History of Cooperative" Citadelle website: https://www.citadelle-camp.coop/maple-syrup/History/1925---1950.aspx

[192] John P. David, "Vermont's Maple Sugar Industry", *The Vermont Review* Vol. 1, No. 6: 139-141 (1927).

[193] "Tuesday Evening Session", *Report of the Proceedings of the Thirty-Fourth Annual Meeting of the Vermont Maple Sugar Makers' Association* (Burlington, VT) 1926, p. 10.

[194] *Maple Sugar and Maple Sirup: Report of the United States Tariff Commission to the President of the United States.* United States Tariff Commission: Government Printing Office (1930).

[195] "Table 2", *Maple Sugar and Maple Sirup: Report of the United States Tariff Commission to the President of the United States.* United States Tariff Commission: Government Printing Office (1930).

[196] "Increased Duty on Maple Sugar Asked," *The Montreal Gazette* (Montreal, Quebec) January 23, 1929; "Vermonters Ask for Higher Tariff On Maple Products," *The Burlington Free Press* (Burlington, VT) January 23, 1929; "Paul E. Sendak "Why the Tariff Failed," *Maple Syrup Digest* Vol. 11, No. 2: 18-22 (1972).

[197] "Tariff On Maple Products," *Report of the Thirty-Fifth Annual Meeting of The Vermont Maple Sugar Makers' Association* (Burlington, VT) 1929.

[198] "Increased Duty on Maple Sugar Asked," *The Montreal Gazette* (Montreal, Quebec) January 23, 1929.

[199] "Maple Sugar Tariff Cut in U.S. Likely," *The Montreal Gazette* (Montreal, Quebec) November 24, 1930.

[200] Paul E. Sendak, The Effect on the Tariff on the Maple Industry, *USDA Forest Service Research Note NE-148*, Northeastern Forest Research Station; Douglas Whynott, *The Sugar Season: A Year in the Life of Maple Syrup, and One Family's Quest for the Sweetest Harvest* (Da Capo Press: Boston, MA) 2014.

[201] "Maple Sugar Tariff Cut in U.S. Likely," *The Montreal Gazette* (Montreal, Quebec) November 24, 1930.

[202] Edward Sherburne Doubleday, "Highlights in the History of the Cary Maple Sugar Co.", *Maple Syrup Digest* vol. 2A, No. 2 (1990).

[203] "Say George C. Cary Bankruptcy Precipitated by Attachment on Property By Burlington Bank," *The Burlington Free* Press (Burlington, VT) September 21, 1931; Nancy Cary Aldrich interview, January 29, 2015.

[204] "Cary Resigns as Maple Sugar Co. Head," *The Burlington Free* Press (Burlington, VT) August 1, 1931; Charlie Welcome, *Cary Maple Sugar Company, St. Johnsbury, Vermont.* Unpublished manuscript, n.d.

[205] "Say George C. Cary Bankruptcy Precipitated by Attachment on Property By Burlington Bank," *The Burlington Free* Press (Burlington, VT) September 21, 1931.

[206] "Maple Sugar King Fails for $3,221,046," *New York Times* (New York, NY) September 19, 1931.

[207] Trustee's Final Report and Account – August 25, 1933. in George C. Cary Papers, Fairbanks Museum Archives (St. Johnsbury, VT).

[208] W.A. Simpson to United Life and Accident Insurance Co. – December 31, 1931, in George C. Cary Papers, Fairbanks Museum Archives (St. Johnsbury, VT).

[209] Trustee's Final Report and Account – August 25, 1933. in George C. Cary Papers, Fairbanks Museum Archives (St. Johnsbury, VT).

[210] "Mrs. Cary Dies In Vermont," *The Berkshire Eagle* (Pittsfield, MA) May 12, 1945; Madeline Cary Fleming, *Biographical Sketch of George and Annie Cary.* George C. Cary Papers, Fairbanks Museum Archives (St. Johnsbury, VT 1976); state of Vermont death records.

[211] Molly Waterman Newell and Joe Newell are presently divorced. Molly Newell operates the Broadview Farm Bed and Breakfast at the Waterman family's historic home, formerly known as Grouselands. Molly Waterman Newell Interview July 8, 2005; Joe Newell Interview July 8, 2005. Marlene "Molly" Newell passed away on June 25, 2015.

[212]. It is assumed, but not known, that the Stanton portion of the sugarbush was also first purchased by Marshall, before being bought by Stanton.

[213] Stephen Jones and Diane Jones Interviews, November 3, 2004 and July 8, 2005.

Chapter Six: A New Empire in a New Era

[214] *The Burlington Free Press* (Burlington, VT) December 16, 1932; "Herbert is Receiver of Cary Maple Co.," *The Burlington Free Press* (Burlington, VT) September 29, 1933.

[215] "Head of Cary Maple Sugar Co. Gets Degree," *The Burlington Free Press* (Burlington, VT) May 29, 1939.

[216] "Southerner Makes a Success of Typical Vermont Industry," *The Burlington Free Press* (Burlington, VT) August 9, 1939.

[217] Personal interview with Charlie Welcome, October 13, 2014.

[218] Charlie Welcome, *Cary Maple Sugar Company, St. Johnsbury, Vermont*. Unpublished manuscript, n.d.

[219] Personal interview with Charlie Welcome, October 13, 2014.

[220] Charlie Welcome, *Cary Maple Sugar Company, St. Johnsbury, Vermont*. Unpublished manuscript, n.d.

[221] Madeline Cary Fleming, *Biographical Sketch of Clinton Partridge Cary*. George C. Cary Papers, Fairbanks Museum Archives (St. Johnsbury, VT 1976); state of Vermont death records

[222] Clare Dunne Johnson, *"I See by the Paper...": An Informal History of St. Johnsbury*, Vol. II (St. Johnsbury, The Cowles Press 1989) 206; *Claire Dunne Johnson papers* – property transaction notes, Fairbanks Museum Archives (St. Johnsbury, VT); Gertrude Franklin died September 5, 1976 with her last address listed as the Bronx, NY, Ancestry.com U.S. Social Security death index.

[223] St. Johnsbury, Vermont City Directory 1948, 1950, 1954; *Maple Products: Investigation into an Alleged Combine in the Purchase of Maple Syrup and maple Sugar in the Province of Quebec*, Report of Commissioner, Combines Investigation Act, Department of Justice, Ottawa (1953).

[224] "Cary Maple Sugar Property Will Be Sold At Auction," *The Burlington Free Press* (Burlington, VT) January 2, 1934.

[225] "New Cary Maple Sugar Co. Buys Out Old Firm," *The Burlington Free Press* (Burlington, VT) February 1, 1934.

[226] "Cary maple Sugar Co. Elects New Officers," *The Burlington Free Press* (Burlington, VT) February 12, 1934.

[227] William H. Jeffery, *Successful Vermonters of Lamoille, Franklin, and Grand Isle Counties*. The Historical Publishing Company. (East Burke, VT) 249-250.

[228] "Clinton P. Cary Dead at 37," *The Burlington Free Press* (Burlington, VT) March 16, 1937; "Throng At Funeral of Clinton P. Cary," *The Burlington Free Press* (Burlington, VT) March 18, 1936.

[229] Clare Dunne Johnson, *"I See by the Paper...": An Informal History of St. Johnsbury*, Vol. II (St. Johnsbury, The Cowles Press 1989) 177.

[230] St. Johnsbury Directory (1931, 1933, 1935, 1939, 1948, 1950, 1954); *Claire Dunne Johnson papers* – property transaction notes, Fairbanks Museum Archives (St. Johnsbury, VT); "For Sale" and" Real Estate," *The Burlington Free Press* (Burlington, VT) April 27, 1937 and May 16, 1941.

[231] "One Time Palatial Fairbanks Home Sold in St. Johnsbury," *The Burlington Free Press* (Burlington, VT) September 3, 1946.

[232] Clare Dunne Johnson, *"I See by the Paper...": An Informal History of St. Johnsbury*, Vol. II (St. Johnsbury, The Cowles Press 1989) 268; Peggy Pearl, "Pinehurst – February 2013 edition of History & Heritage," St. Johnsbury History and Heritage Center blog, February 20, 2013, http://stjhistory.org/wordpress/?p=587; National Register of Historic Places Inventory Nomination Form – St. Johnsbury Main Street Historic District, April 17, 1975.

[233] Edward Sherburne Doubleday, "Highlights in the History of the Cary Maple Sugar Co.", *Maple Syrup Digest* vol. 2A, No. 2 (1990).

[234] *Maple Products: Investigation into an Alleged Combine in the Purchase of Maple Syrup and maple Sugar in the Province of Quebec*, Report of Commissioner, Combines Investigation Act, Department of Justice, Ottawa (1953).

[235] *Maple Products: Investigation into an Alleged Combine in the Purchase of Maple Syrup and maple Sugar in the Province of Quebec*, Report of Commissioner, Combines Investigation Act, Department of Justice, Ottawa (1953).

[236] The four classifications or markets noted by Boylan were tobacco industry, blending industry, flavoring industry, and direct consumption. Edward R. Boylan, "Economic Trends in Maple Sirup – Production and Sales", *Report of Proceedings – Third Conference on Maple Products*, Eastern Utilization Research Branch, Agricultural Research Service, U.S. Department of Agriculture (Philadelphia, PA) 1956.

[237] Charlie Welcome, *Cary Maple Sugar Company, St. Johnsbury, Vermont*. Unpublished manuscript, n.d.

[238] Charlie Welcome, *Cary Maple Sugar Company, St. Johnsbury, Vermont*. Unpublished manuscript, n.d.

[239] Charlie Welcome, *Cary Maple Sugar Company, St. Johnsbury, Vermont*. Unpublished manuscript, n.d.

[240] Charlie Welcome, *Cary Maple Sugar Company, St. Johnsbury, Vermont*. Unpublished manuscript, n.d.

[241] "Preston Herbert is Dead at 70," *The Burlington Free Press* (Burlington, VT) December 1, 1941; "W. Arthur Simpson Heads Cary Maple Sugar Co. Directors," *The Burlington Free Press* (Burlington, VT) February 7, 1942; "Cary Maple Sugar Co. Officers Are Elected," *The Burlington Free Press* (Burlington, VT) May 6, 1942.

[242] "Cary Maple Co. Returns to Private Ownership Again," *The Burlington Free Press* (Burlington, VT) September 24, 1943; "Under Local Control," *The Burlington Free Press* (Burlington, VT) October 16, 1943.

[243] "Cary Maple Sugar Company Elects," *The Burlington Free Press* (Burlington, VT) May 23, 1945.

244 "The Cary Maple Sugar Company of St. Johnsbury Introduces Agricultural Industry to Vt. – Apple Syrup," *The Burlington Free Press* (Burlington, VT) May 11, 1943; "Maple Sugar Company Makes Trial Run of Apple Juice; To Report Here Today," *The Burlington Free Press* (Burlington, VT) June 29, 1943; "Cary Maple Sugar Company to Abandon Commercial Manufacture of Apple Syrup Apples are Needed for Consumption," *The Burlington Free Press* (Burlington, VT) August 26, 1943; Clare Dunne Johnson, *"I See by the Paper…": An Informal History of St. Johnsbury*, Vol. II (St. Johnsbury, The Cowles Press 1989) 258.

245 "'Better' Maple Syrup in Making," *Ogdensburg Journal* (Ogdensburg, NY) February 10, 1949.

246 "Cary Maple Sugar Co. Sold to Boston Firm," *The Burlington Free Press* (Burlington, VT) October 4, 1947; Clare Dunne Johnson, *"I See by the Paper…": An Informal History of St. Johnsbury*, Vol. II (St. Johnsbury, The Cowles Press 1989) 312.

247 "Arthur Simpson Resigns as a Director of Maple Sugar Co.," *The Burlington Free Press* (Burlington, VT) October 2, 1947.

248 Clare Dunne Johnson, *"I See by the Paper…": An Informal History of St. Johnsbury*, Vol. II (St. Johnsbury, The Cowles Press 1989) 395; A.B. Moore, History of the Crop of 1953, Cary Maple Sugar Company, Manuscript in Private Collections of Tom Olson, Rutland, VT.

249 Charlie Welcome, *Cary Maple Sugar Company, St. Johnsbury, Vermont*. Unpublished manuscript, n.d.

250 "St. Johnsbury Maple Candy Concern Sold," *The Burlington Free Press* (Burlington, VT) September 18, 1953; Charlie Welcome, *Cary Maple Sugar Company, St. Johnsbury, Vermont*. Unpublished manuscript, n.d.

251 "Whaley Buys Maple Grove, Retaining Local Industry," *Caledonian* (St. Johnsbury, VT) September 17, 1953; The Maple Museum opened its doors on May 1, 1953 according to Whaley.

252 Stephen Jones shared that he was told that the sugar house was previously located in the woods of what is today the St. Johnsbury Academy property, formerly the Zabarsky lands, and before that Cary's Highland Farm in North Danville, and that it as an unused and very weathered relic, was dismantled and rebuilt in in St. Johnsbury in the 1950s. Personal communication February 2018.

253 Clare Dunne Johnson, *"I See by the Paper…": An Informal History of St. Johnsbury*, Vol. II (St. Johnsbury, The Cowles Press 1989) 386.

254 "Maple Candy Business is feature attraction for Summer Visitors," *Caledonian Record* (St. Johnsbury, VT) July 28, 1953, p. 4; Clare Dunne Johnson, *"I See by the Paper…": An Informal History of St. Johnsbury*, Vol. II (St. Johnsbury, The Cowles Press 1989) 436.

255 "Harold Whaley, 'Candy King'," *The Burlington Free Press* (Burlington, VT) July 27, 1955.

256 Charlie Welcome, *Cary Maple Sugar Company, St. Johnsbury, Vermont*. Unpublished manuscript, n.d.

257 "Childs Buys Fear & Co.," *New York Times* (New York, NY) August 5, 1954.

258 "Cary Maple Co. Sold to Childs Restaurant Chain," *The Burlington Free Press* (Burlington, VT) August 4, 1954

259 History of the Crop Annual Reports 1953, 1954, 1955, 1956, 1957, 1966, 1967– Cary Maple Sugar Company. Manuscript in Private Collections of Tom Olson, Rutland, VT.

261 Correspondence Related to NRHP Eligibility of Maple Grove / Cary Maple Sugar Company, St. Johnsbury, VT, Vermont Division for Historic Preservation (February 23, March 28, April 4 1984).

262 Francis R Kowsky, "Statement of Significance for M. Wile Factory, Buffalo, New York," National Register of Historic Places Nomination Form.

263 "Maple Grove Farms of Vermont." International Directory of Company Histories. (February 22, 2017).http://www.encyclopedia.com/books/politics-and-business-magazines/maple-grove-farms-vermont; B & G Foods, incorporated, 2015 Annual Report.

264 Maple Grove Turns 100, *Caledonian Record* (St. Johnsbury, VT) July 23, 2015.

Chapter Seven: Legacy of a Maple King

265 David K. Leff, "Maple Sugaring: Keeping It Real In New England", (Middletown, CT, Wesleyan University Press, 2015), p. 70.

266 Madeline Cary Fleming, "Cary & Partridge Family Biographies, Written 1976-77 for my four nieces", George C. Cary Papers, St. Johnsbury Historical Society

267 "Harold Whaley, 'Candy King'," *The Burlington Free Press* (Burlington, VT) July 27, 1955.

268 National Register of Historic Places Inventory Nomination Form – St. Johnsbury Main Street Historic District, April 17, 1975.

Made in the USA
Middletown, DE
03 October 2018